PENSIONERS OF REVOLUTIONARY WAR STRUCK OFF THE ROLL

●

With an Added

INDEX TO STATES

CLEARFIELD

Originally Published
Washington, 1836

Reprinted with an added Index to States
Genealogical Publishing Company
Baltimore, 1969

Reprinted for
Clearfield Company, Inc. by
Genealogical Publishing Co., Inc.
Baltimore, Maryland
1989, 1993, 1998, 2002

Library of Congress Catalogue Card Number 71-78506
International Standard Book Number: 0-8063-0350-6

Copyright © 1969
Genealogical Publishing Company
Baltimore, Maryland
All rights reserved

Made in the United States of America

Index To States

	Pages
Alabama	91
Connecticut	50- 58
Delaware	80
District of Columbia	82
Georgia	91
Illinois	102
Indiana	101
Kentucky	92- 94
Louisiana	103
Maine	2- 13
Maryland	81
Massachusetts	31- 48
Michigan	102
Mississippi	102
Missouri	103
New Hampshire	14- 21
New Jersey	72- 74
New York	59- 71
North Carolina	87- 88
Ohio	95- 98
Pennsylvania	75- 79
Rhode Island	49
South Carolina	89- 90
Tennessee	99-100
Vermont	22- 30
Virginia	83- 86

24th Congress, [Doc. No. 127.] Ho. of Reps.
1st Session.   War Dept.

PENSIONERS OF REVOLUTIONARY WAR—STRUCK OFF THE ROLL.

LETTER

FROM

THE SECRETARY OF WAR,

TRANSMITTING

A list of the names of pensioners, under the act of 18th of March, 1818, whose names were struck of the list by act of 1st May, 1820, and subsequently restored, &c. &c.

FEBRUARY 25, 1836.
Read, and laid upon the table.

WAR DEPARTMENT, *February 25, 1836.*

SIR: I have the honor to enclose a report of the commissioner of pensions, in answer to the resolution of the House of Representatives of December 17, 1835.
Very respectfully,
Your most obedient servant,
LEW: CASS.

Hon. JAMES K. POLK,
Speaker of the House of Reps.

WAR DEPARTMENT,
Pension Office, *February 24, 1836.*

SIR: In compliance with your instructions, requiring me to furnish, in obedience to the resolution of the House of Representatives, of the 17th December last, "a statement of the names of all the pensioners for services during the revolutionary war, pensioned under the act of Congress of the 18th of March, 1818, whose names were struck off the list, by virtue of the act of the 1st of May, 1820, specifying those restored to pensions by the act of 1st March, 1823, or since, again pensioned under the act of the 15th of May, 1828, the act of the 7th of June, 1832, or any other act of Congress subsequent to that of the 1st of May, 1820." I have the honor to transmit herewith lists of the names of all the persons embraced by that resolution, with such explanatory remarks as are deemed necessary to a proper understanding of the subject.
I have the honor to be,
Very respectfully, sir,
Your most obedient servant,
J. L. EDWARDS,
Com'r of Pensions.

Hon. LEWIS CASS,
Secretary of War.

Blair & Rives, printers.

[Doc. No. 127.]

A STATEMENT of the names of all the pensioners for services during the revolutionary war, pensioned under the act of Congress of the 18th March, 1818, whose names were struck off by virtue of the act of 1st May, 1820, specifying those restored to pensions by the act of 1st March, 1823, or since again pensioned under the act of 15th May, 1828, the act of June 7, 1832, or any other act of Congress subsequent to that of the 1st May, 1820, prepared in conformity with a resolution of the House of Representatives of the United States of the 17th December, 1835.

PENSIONERS in Maine who have been dropped from the pension roll under the act of 1st May, 1820, prepared in conformity with the resolution of the House of Representatives of the 17th December, 1835.

Names.	Acts under which restored.	Remarks.
Job Allen	June 7, 1832	
Isaac Allen	do.	
Daniel Allen, 1st	do.	
Moses Ayer		
Samuel Adams	do.	
Daniel Allen, 2d	March 1, 1823	
Jacob Allen	June 7, 1832	
Joel Atherton	March 1, 1823	
John Atherton	June 7, 1832	
William Andrews	do.	
John Abbott	do.	
James Allen	March 1, 1823	
Jonah Austin	June 7, 1832	
Henry Abbott	March 1, 1823	
Simeon Applebee	June 7, 1832	
Samuel Andrews	do.	
Amos Allen	do.	
Benjamin Austin		
Joel Adams		
Ephraim Alley	March 1, 1823	
Jeremiah Andrews	do.	
Jacob Allen, 2d	June 7, 1832	
Nathan Atwood	March 1, 1823	
Nathaniel Abbott	do.	
Daniel Abbott	June 7, 1832	
Jedediah Adams	March 1, 1823	
Samuel Baker		
William Boothby		
Joseph Besse	do.	
Joseph Blake	do.	
Jeremiah Bettes	June 7, 1832	
Daniel Barker		
George Berry	do.	
Josiah Berry	March 1, 1823	
Humphrey Burrell	do.	Relinquished for an increase of his stipend under the act of the 7th of June, 1832.
Timothy Blanchard	do.	Relinquished for an increase of his stipend under the act of the 7th of June, 1832.
Jonathan Ballard	do.	
Jonathan Burgess	do.	
Jeremiah Babcock		
Ezekiel Brown		
Josiah Bean	June 7, 1832	
Eleazer Burbank	do.	
David Burgess	do.	
David Bennett	March 1, 1823	

PENSIONERS IN MAINE—Continued.

Names.	Acts under which restored.	Remarks.
David Burr	June 7, 1832	
Joab Black		
Abner Briggs	do.	
William Barrows	do.	
John Bridgham	do.	
John Burbank	do.	
Thomas Baston	do.	
Daniel Barnard		
John Brackett	do.	
Arthur Bragdon	do.	
Samuel Benjamin		
Peabody Bradford	do.	
John Blake	do.	
Abraham Barnes		
Gideon Bacheldor		
Melzar Byram		
Samuel Barker		
Joshua Bailey		
John Bean	Invalid roll	Restored under the 3d section of the act of the 1st of May, 1820.
Peter Barrows	Invalid	Restored under the 3d section of the act of the 1st of May, 1820. Again restored under the act of the 1st of March, 1823.
Samuel Brown	June 7, 1832	
Malachi Bartlett	March 1, 1823	
John Baxter	do.	
Benjamin Barstow		
Levi Bowker	do.	
Elijah Boston	June 7, 1832	
Jonathan Byram	do.	
Theophilus Blancher		
Prince Bailey	March 1, 1823	
Eliphalet Bailey	June 7, 1832	
Willing Blake	do.	
John Barter		
Benjamin Butman	do.	
Joseph Burr	March 1, 1823	
Solomon Barber	do.	
Nathan Barnard		
John Beeman		
Timothy Bacon	March 1, 1823	
Isaac Bussell	May 15, 1828	
Ebenezer Byram	June 7, 1832	
Ebenezer Booden		
Elijah Bradford	March 1, 1823	
Jesse Brown	do.	
James Barker	do.	
Isaiah Cushman	June 7, 1832	
Benjamin Cox	March 1, 1823	
Ebenezer Choate	June 7, 1832	
Eli Cole	do.	
Ebenezer Cousins		
Charles Church	do.	
Lemuel Collins	March 1, 1823	
Andrew Cushman	June 7, 1832	
John Cole		
Abijah Crane	do.	
Benjamin Chase		
Robert Cofren	do.	
James Campbell	March 1, 1823	
Michael Crowell	do.	
Benjamin Clough	June 7, 1832	

[Doc. No. 127.]

PENSIONERS IN MAINE—Continued.

Names.	Acts under which restored.	Remarks.
Daniel Collins, 1st	June 7, 1832	
Moses Chandler	May 15, 1828	
John Chandler	June 7, 1832	
John Cheney	March 1, 1823	
Moses Chandler		
Joshua Crooker		
Samuel Cole	do.	
Jonathan Clark		
Josiah Chute	Invalid	Restored under the 3d section of the act of the 1st of May, 1820.
William Chipman	June 7, 1832	
Jabes Churchill	March 1, 1823	
Thomas Chase	June 7, 1832	
Moses Chamberlain	March 1, 1823	
Josiah Clark	June 7, 1832	
John Cash	do.	
David Cain	March 1, 1823	
Daniel Chaplin		
Benjamin Conant	June 7, 1832	
Joseph Cook	March 1, 1823	
James Clark, 2d		
Ezekiel Chase	May 15, 1828	
David Chaplin	June 7, 1832	
John Cool	do.	
Elias Craig	do.	
Sylvanus Cobb		
Joseph S. Coombs	do.	
Thomas Crawford	do.	
David Colson	May 20, 1830	
Samuel Cammett		
David Clark	May 15, 1828	
Daniel Collins, 2d	June 7, 1832	
Ephraim Clark	do.	
Benjamin Clay		
Ephraim Chamberlain	March 1, 1823	
Joseph Crary	June 7, 1832	
Isaac Cowan	March 1, 1823	
Thomas Davis, 1st	June 7, 1832	
Edmund Dean	do.	
Richard Dresser	March 1, 1823	
John Downing	do.	
Joshua Davis	do.	
David Dennison	June 7, 1832	
Philip Davis	do.	
Christopher Dunn	do.	
Simon Dearborn, jr.	March 1, 1823	
Benjamin Dolbear	do.	
Tristram Daggett	May 20, 1830	
Thomas Decker	March 1, 1823	
William Davis	do.	
Samuel Davis	June 7, 1832	
Sanford Davis	March 1, 1823	
Amos Dole	do.	
Moses Dunham	June 7, 1832	
Israel Derman	do.	
Stephen Dodd	March 1, 1823	
Ebenezer Dennett	June 7, 1832	
Joseph Dennett	do	
Isaac Dyer, 2d	do.	
John Davis	March 1, 1823	
Nathaniel Day, 2d	do.	
James Doughty, 2d	June 7, 1832	

[Doc. No. 127.] 5

PENSIONERS IN MAINE—Continued.

Names.	Acts under which restored.	Remarks.
Jonathan Delano	March 1, 1823	
Abner Danforth	do.	
Obadiah Donnell		
William Davis, 3d	do.	
David Dunbar	June 7, 1832	
Paul Dodge		
Jotham Donnell		
Nathaniel Doughty or Doty		
Nathan Dudley	do.	
David Davis	do.	
Aaron Davis	do.	
Paul Downs	do.	
Amos Doane	March 1, 1823	
David Emery	do.	
William Eaton	June 7, 1832	
Josiah Everett	March 1, 1823	
Ebenezer Eaton	June 7, 1832	
James Edgcomb	do.	
Jedediah Elliot	do.	
Job Emery	do.	
Gibeon Elden	do.	
Samuel Eames	do.	
Henry Flood	March 1, 1823	
Elijah Fisher	do.	
Elias Fosse	June 7, 1832	
Mark Frost	March 1, 1823	
George Fogg	June 7, 1832	
John Fifield	May 15, 1828	
Zachariah Foss	June 7, 1832	
Samuel File	do.	
Ebenezer File	do.	
John Fletcher	do.	
Thomas Flint		
William Fairfield		
Elliott Frost	do.	
Jacob Fisher	do.	
Ebenezer Fisher	do.	
Joseph Freethy	March 1, 1823	
Barzilla Fuller	May 15, 1828	
Dennis Fernald	June 7, 1832	
Jonathan Ferren		
John Fitzgerald	March 1, 1823	
George Fall	May 15, 1828	
David Fitzgerald		
Enoch Fuller	March 1, 1823	
John Farrow	June 7, 1832	
Pelatiah Fenderson	do.	
Joseph Felker	March 1, 1823	
John Faxon		
John Flanders		
Simeon Fish	do.	
John Guilford, jr.	do.	
Philip Goldthwaite	May 15, 1828	
Samuel Gedding	March 1, 1823	
Joseph Gillpatrick	June 7, 1832	
Martin Grant		
Timothy Golthwaite	do.	
Francis George	March 1, 1823	
John Greenleaf	June 7, 1832	
Daniel Gale	do.	
Nathaniel Gillpatrick	March 1, 1823	
Stephen Googins	do.	

PENSIONERS IN MAINE—Continued.

Names.	Acts under which restored.	Remarks.
Daniel Gage	March 1, 1823	
Adam Goodwin	June 7, 1832	
George Goodwin	March 1, 1823	
Samuel Gilmore	June 7, 1832	
Joseph Gordon	May 15, 1828	
Alexander Goold	June 7, 1832	
Jedediah Gooch	do.	
James Gillpatrick	do.	
Benjamin Gatchell	March 1, 1823	
John Given	June 7, 1832	
Simeon Goodwin	do.	
Reuben Goodwin		
Joshua Grant	March 1, 1823	
James Gilkey		
Reuben Goodwin, jr.	June 7, 1832	
Daniel Gould	do.	
Patrick Grace		
Amos Gage	do.	
Benjamin Gross	do.	
Jonathan Green	March 1, 1823	
Benjamin Goodwin		
Noah Greeley	June 7, 1832	
Richard Goodwin	do.	
Jeremiah Hill		
William Hamilton	do.	
Gershom Holmes	do.	
Pelatiah Harmon	do.	
Daniel Hill	do.	
Thomas Harmon	do.	
William Harmon	March 1, 1823	
Jonathan Hanson		
Ebenezer Hilton, 1st	do.	
Benjamin Horsum	do.	
Benjamin Hinds	do.	
Nehemiah Hutchinson	do.	
Charles Harris	do.	
Ebenezer Hilton, 2d	June 7, 1832	
Ichabod Hunt		
Nathaniel House	March 1, 1823	
Israel Hutchinson	June 7, 1832	
William Hilton	do.	
Stephen Hollis		
William Haskell		
Solomon Hallett	do.	
Elijah Hackett		
Ward Haskell		
America Hamlin	do.	
Benjamin Hale	do.	
Edward Hilton	June 7, 1832	
Stephen Hardison		
Ephraim Hathaway	do.	
Israel Hale	do.	
Jonathan Holmes	May 15, 1828	
William Harvey	June 7, 1832	
David Horsum	do.	
Josiah Hobbs	do.	
Samuel Hicks	do.	
Timothy Hudson	March 1, 1823	
William Heath	Invalid	Restored under the 3d section of the act of the 1st of May, 1820. Also on the roll under the act of the 15th of May, 1828, conformably to the provisions of the act of the 31st of May, 1830.

[Doc. No. 127.] 7

PENSIONERS IN MAINE—Continued.

Names.	Acts under which restored.	Remarks.
Eastman Hutchins		
Jonathan Horn	March 1, 1823	
Christian Hoofses	June 7, 1832	
William Hilton, 2d	do.	
Daniel Holden	May 15, 1828	
Enoch Hall	June 7, 1832	
Joseph Hilton	do.	
Edmund Hagins	do.	
Samuel Houston	do.	
Judah Hackett		
Charles Havenor	do.	
Reuben Hanscom		
Jacob Hart	March 1, 1823	
Nehemiah Hinkley	June 7, 1832	
Elnathan Handy	March 1, 1823	
Nathaniel Harlow		
John Hart	June 7, 1832	
Elijah Hatch	March 1, 1823	
Richard Heath	June 7, 1832	
Joseph Howard	do.	
John Harris	March 1, 1823	
David Jones		
Hezekiah Jordon		
Eliphalet Jennings	do.	
Amos Jones	do.	
John Jacobs	do.	
David Ingham	do.	
Samuel Jenkins	do.	Relinquished for an increase of his stipend, under the act of the 7th of June, 1832.
Joshua Jones	June 7, 1832	
Nathaniel Jackson		
Elijah Jordan	March 1, 1823	
John Jewell, 2d	do.	
Lemuel Jenkins	do.	Relinquished for an increase of his stipend, under the act of the 7th of June, 1832.
Thomas Jones		
Philip Judkins	do.	
Joseph Jackson, 2d		
Moses Jewett		
Thomas Jordon		
Elijah Kellogg	June 7, 1832	
Jonathan Knight	do.	
Joseph Kelley		
John Kilborn	May 15, 1828	
Mehach Keene	June 7, 1832	
Daniel Kinsley	March 1, 1823	
Ebenezer Keyes	June 7, 1832	
Joseph Kilgore	March 1, 1823	
Ichabod King		
David Knox	do.	
John Kingsbury		
James Keene	do.	
William Kendall		
Benjamin Kimball	June 7, 1832	
Simon Knowles	May 15, 1828	
William Keene		
Joseph Knowlton	June 7, 1832	
David Kezer	March 1, 1823	
Thomas Knowlton		
David Kenniston	May 15, 1828	
Francis Libby	June 7, 1832	
Ezriah Libby		

PENSIONERS IN MAINE—Continued.

Names.	Acts under which restored.	Remarks.
Solomon Libby	March 1, 1823	
William Libby	June 7, 1832	
Elias Lord	March 1, 1823	
Caleb Lumbard	do.	
Thomas Libby		
James Lord	do.	
Samuel Longfellow	do.	
Edward Leavett		
Nathaniel Lombard	June 7, 1832	
Asa Longley	do.	
Zebulon Libby	do.	
John Lincoln		
Wentworth Lord	March 1, 1823	
Joseph Leland	May 15, 1828	
Joseph Lineken		
Nathan Lord	June 7, 1832	
Richard Lord	do.	
Johnson Littlefield		
Edward Libby	do.	
Ichabod Lord	do.	
Isaac Lawrence	do.	
John Lawrence	do.	
Amos Lunt	do.	
Paul Lowell	March 1, 1823	
James Lara	do.	
Nathaniel Libby	June 7, 1832	
William Leavett	do.	
Joseph Lord		
Elisha Lord		
Daniel Littlefield	do.	
Benjamin Lowell	May, 15, 1828	
Increase Leadbetter	March 1, 1823	
Simeon Libby		
George Leach	do.	
Daniel Lord, 3d		
Josiah Lovell		
Joseph Lewis	June 7, 1832	
Harvey Libby	do.	
Shubael Luce		
Jacob Lewey	March 1, 1823	
John Low		
Dyre Lammas	do.	
Jonathan Low	June 7, 1832	
Robert Libbee	do.	
Joseph Leavett	do.	
Richard H. Libby		
Levi Morse	do.	
Simeon Moulton	do.	
Lemuel Miller	March 1, 1823	Relinqushed for an increase of his stipend under the act of the 7th of June, 1832.
Jacob Merrill	June 7, 1832	
Phineas McIntire	do.	
Noah Marsh	March 1, 1823	
David Marston	June 7, 1832	
Theodore Marston		
Solomon McFarlin		
Philip Morse	do.	
Thomas Means, 2d	March 1, 1823	
Abner Millikin		
Isaac Moores	June 7, 1832	
John McIntosh	do.	
George Moody	March 1, 1823	

[Doc. No. 127.]

PENSIONERS IN MAINE—Continued.

Names.	Acts under which restored.	Remarks.
Josiah Moses	June 7, 1832	
David Morton		
Benjamin Moore	March 1, 1823	
James Murdock	June 7, 1832	
James Means	May 15, 1828	
William Maxwell	March 1, 1823	
William Mallet	June 7, 1832	
John Moody	do.	
William Merritt	March 1, 1823	
Thomas Murphy, 2d	June 7, 1832	
James Morrison	do.	
Jonathan Moors		
James Morton	do.	
Thomas Morton	do.	
Robert Maxfield	March 1, 1823	
Aaron Moosman	June 7, 1832	
Richard McAlister	do.	
Solomon Meserve	March 1, 1823	
Abijah Munroe		
John More		
John Norman		
Edward Nason	June 7, 1832	
Zachariah Nowell	do.	
Mark Nowell	do.	
Jonathan Nork	do.	
George Newbiggen	do.	
Moses Norwood	March 1, 1823	
Paul Nickerson		
Thomas Neal	June 7, 1832	
Nathaniel Norton		
Samuel Nichols	March 1, 1823	
James Osborne	June 7, 1832	
Philip Owen	do.	
Jonathan Oliver	do.	
John Obrian	do.	
Thaddeus Pratt	March 1, 1823	
Joseph Perkins	June 7, 1832	
James Pearce	May 15, 1828	
William Payne	March 1, 1823	
Caleb Page		
Edmund Parker	June 7, 1832	
Jarius Phillips		
Ichabod Phillips		
David Paul	March 1, 1823	
William Pullen		
Calvin Pinkham	June 7, 1832	
William Plummer	March 1, 1823	
Samuel Pray	June 7, 1832	
George Pratt	March 1, 1823	
John Pierce		
Benjamin Penny	June 7, 1832	
Philip Page		
Benjamin J. Porter	May 15, 1828	
Thomas Paine	June 7, 1832	
John Plaisted	do.	
Nathan Pillsbury	March 1, 1823	
Samuel Prescott	do.	
William Pickett	June 7, 1832	
Norton Phillips	do.	
Barnabas Parker	March 1, 1823	
Matthew Pettengill	June 7, 1832	
William Perkins		

[Doc. No. 127.]
PENSIONERS IN MAINE—Continued.

Names.	Acts under which restored.	Remarks.
John Penny	March 1, 1823	
Nathaniel Palmer	June 7, 1832	
Samuel Payson	May 20, 1830	
Isaac Plummer		
John Phinney	March 1, 1823	
Joseph Phinney		
James Perkins		
Stephen Peavy or Pearce	June 7, 1832	
Bezaleel Palmer		
Daniel Plummer	March 1, 1823	
Abijah Poole		
Isaac Pope		
Joseph Pulcifer		
Josiah Parker	June 7, 1832	
John Robinson		
Joseph Richards	do.	
Daniel Robbins	March 1, 1823	
George Ridley		
Daniel Ridley	do.	
Joseph Rice	do.	
Asa Robbins	June 7, 1832	
Stephen Ridout	March 1, 1823	
Eliphalet Robbins	do.	
Gideon Rice	June 7, 1832	
George Ricker	March 1, 1823	
Luther Rice	do.	
Jonathan Robbins		
Maturian Ricker	June 7, 1832	
Reuben Ricker	May 20, 1830	
John Rowe		
Abraham Reed	March 1, 1823	
Benjamin Rowe	do.	
James Rendall		
Isaac Ross	June 7, 1832	
Samuel Roberts		
Noah Ricker	do.	
Daniel Robbins, 2d		
Ebenezer Redlon	March 1, 1823	
Dominicus Rumner	June 7, 1832	
Love Roberts	March 1, 1823	
Joseph Roberts	June 7, 1832	
Joseph Ryant	do.	
William Robbins		
Levi Russell	March 1, 1823	
Samuel Remick		
Benjamin Radford		
Samuel Randall	June 7, 1832	
Nathan Swan	March 1, 1823	
Charles Sargent	do.	
James Stanley		
Elisha Skinner	do.	
Micah Stockbridge	June 7, 1832	
Zachariah Small		
John Sanborne		
Ephraim Stinchfield	do.	
John Swett	do.	
Paul Sanborn		
John Stone	do.	
Ebenezer Smith		
John Smith, 2d	do.	
George Stone	do.	
William Sawyer	do.	

[Doc. No. 127.] 11

PENSIONERS IN MAINE—Continued.

Names.	Acts under which restored.	Remarks.
Elisha Small		
Dominicus Smith	March 1, 1823	
William Symmes	Invalid	Restored under the 3d section of the act of the 1st of May, 1820.
Jonathan Somers		
Henry Sewall	May 15, 1828	
Samuel Stowers	June 7, 1832	
James Shepard		
William Stacy	March 1, 1823	
Nathaniel Stoddard		
Benjamin Sanborn	June 7, 1832	
Nathaniel Sayer	do.	
Benjamin Silly	March 1, 1823	
Nathan Smith	do.	
Joshua Severance	June 7, 1832	
Benjamin Sanborn, 2d		
Ebenezer Sawyer	do.	
Henry Small		
Abraham Shaw	do.	
Isaac Storer	do.	
Laban Smith	do.	
John Sawyer		
Eliakim Sevey	March 1, 1823	
Joseph F. Swan	June 7, 1832	
Daniel Small	do.	
Jonathan Stone	do.	
Jonas Stevens	do.	
Hezekiah Stetson	do.	
William Smith	May 15, 1828	
Seth Sturtevant	March 1, 1823	
James Small	June 7, 1832	
Joseph Shackley	do.	
Samuel Sprague	do.	
Andrew Sturtevant	March 1, 1823	
William Sprague		
Adin Stanley	June 7, 1832	
Amasa Steward	do.	
Lot Sturtevant	March 1, 1823	
James Snow	do.	
Francis Soucee		
William Stinson		
Richard Sweetser	do.	
Batchelor Stetson		
William Spaulding	June 7, 1832	
Matthew N. Sanborn	March 1, 1823	
Charles Smith	do.	
Jonas Sawtell		
Joshua Swett	June 7, 1832	
Nathaniel Shaw		
Jasiel Smith	do.	
Thomas Shaw	do.	
Nathaniel Seger	do.	
Daniel Small, 2d	do.	
Ebenezer Symmes		
James Smith	March 1, 1823	
Joshua Snow	May 15, 1828	
Enoch Spurr	June 7, 1832	
Paul Dudley Sargeant	March 1, 1823	
Benjamin Shaw		
John Staples		
Caleb Spinney		
Thomas Stevens		

PENSIONERS IN MAINE—Continued.

Names.	Acts under which restored.	Remarks.
Elijah Stetson		
Benjamin Simpson	June 7, 1832	
Josiah Spaulding	do.	
Noah Smith	May 5, 1823	Special act.
Joseph Townsend		
Nathaniel Thing	June 7, 1832	
Jacob Tubbs		
Jacob Thurston		
Joseph Tyler		
James Thompson	do.	
William Thompson	March 1, 1823	
Joseph Tarbell		
Jeremiah Thayer		
Noah Towne	do.	
Joseph Tarr		
Michael Tappan	do.	
Joseph Thomas or Thombs	June 7, 1832	
Josiah Trafton		
David Turner	March 1, 1823	
Andrew Tyler	June 7, 1832	
Joshua Thomas		
Masters Treadwell		
Benjamin Trafton		
Thomas Trask, jr.	March 1, 1823	
Ephraim Taylor	do.	
Samuel Tobin	do.	
Philip Thayer		
Charles Thomas	June 7, 1832	
Joseph Thompson	do.	
Robert Thompson		
Jacob Townsly	do.	
Eliphalet Trafton		
John Tibbetts	March 1, 1823	
James Uran		
Jeduthan Upton		
John Varner		
John Vining	June 7, 1832	
Thomas Worster		
Jonathan Whitney		
John Wheeler	March 1, 1823	
Josiah Wyer		
Daniel Weston	do.	
Joseph Wardwell	do.	
Ephraim Woodman		
John Whitten		
Thomas Ward		
Isaac Whitney, 1st	do.	Relinquished for an increase of his stipend, under the act of the 7th of June, 1832.
Abraham Whitney	do.	
John Walker		
Obadiah Witherell	June 7, 1832	
Lemuel Williams		
Benjamin Woodward		
Robert Withington	March 1, 1823	
Daniel Wyman, 1st		
Daniel Whitmore	do.	
Richard Warren	do.	
John Wilson	do.	
Samuel Whitney	June 7, 1832	
William Welch	March 1, 1823	
Lewis Webber	June 7, 1832	
John Whitehouse		

[Doc. No. 127.]   13

PENSIONERS IN MAINE—Continued.

Names.	Acts under which restored.	Remarks.
Joseph Wight	June 7, 1832	
Edward Webb	March 1, 1823	
Joshua Warren	June 7, 1832	
Daniel Warren	do.	
William Wait	do.	
Isaac West	do.	
Nathan Wing	March 1, 1823	
Zoe Withee	do.	
Jesse Wood	do.	
Benjamin Woodbury		
Jeremiah Weare	June 7, 1832	
Benjamin Webber		
Aaron Warren		
John Woodman		
Stephen Webber	do.	
Asa Webber	do.	
John Wadsworth	do.	
Daniel Wadlia		
William Wocester	March 1, 1823	
Joseph White	June 7, 1832	
Benjamin Williams		
James Weymouth	do.	
Uriel Whitney	do.	
Isaac Whitney, 2d	do.	
Charles Walck		
William Weston	March 1, 1823	
Joseph Wellman		
Jesse Wedgwood	June 7, 1832	
Daniel Whitney	do.	
Daniel Webber	March 1, 1823	
Nathan Wood		
Phineas Wiggin		
William Webber		
Thomas Wasson	June 7, 1832	
John Wasson	do.	
Samuel Woodsum	do.	
Sampson Whiting	do.	
Silas Winchester	March 1, 1823	
John Wentworth, 2d		
Joseph Waterhouse	June 7, 1832	
Daniel Whitehouse	March 1, 1823	
Andrew Wentworth		
Peter Warren	do.	
Nathaniel Young	June 7, 1832	
William Ring York	do.	
Isaac York	do.	
Isaac York, 2d	do	
Zebulon Young	do.	

PENSIONERS in New Hampshire who have been dropped from the pension roll under the Act of 1st May, 1820, prepared in conformity with the resolution of the House of Representatives of the 17th December, 1835.

Names.	Acts under which restored.	Remarks.
Moses Austin	March 1, 1823	
John Adams	May 15, 1828	
Moses Abbott	June 7, 1832	
Jeremiah Abbott		
Allen Anderson	do	
Thomas Applebee	do	
Solomon Ames	March 1, 1823	
Beriah Abbott		
Theodore Atkinson	May 15, 1828	
Joel Adams	March 1, 1823	
Ebenezer Adams	do	
Ezra Abbott	do	
Joses Buckman	do	
Thomas Blood	do	
Jonathan Bachelder	do	
Selden Border	do	
Levi Blood	June 7, 1832	
Amos Brooks	March 1, 1823	
William Burleigh	do	
Benjamin Bean	do	
James Burnham	do	Relinquished for an increase of his stipend under the act of June 7, 1832.
Nathaniel Bootman		
Samuel Buss	do	
Samuel Bickford		
John Burnham	do	Relinquished for an increase of his stipend under the act of May 15, 1828.
Benjamin Butler		
Samuel Ball	June 7, 1832	
Nathan Bent	March 1, 1823	
Oliver Bacon	May 15, 1828	
James Bemis	March 1, 1823	
Eleazer Blake	May 15, 1828	
William Bradford	June 7, 1832	
Nathan Brown	March 1, 1823	
Jonas Blodget	Invalid roll	Restored to invalid roll under the 3d section of the act of the 1st of May, 1820.
John Brewster		
William Bond	June 7, 1832	
Michael Barstow	March 1, 1823	
John Barker		
Nathaniel Bartlett	June 7, 1832	
Ammi Burnham		
Moses Brewer		
Benjamin Brown, 2d		
Lemuel Barrett	June 7, 1832	
Lemuel Blood	do	
Abijah Brown	March 1, 1823	
John Balch	do	
Jacob Bixby		
Francis Barker		
Samuel Barron	June 7, 1832	
Amos Blood	do	
Jonathan Buzzell		
Nathan Bolster		
William Burrows, 2d		
John Brooks	do	

[Doc. No. 127] 15

PENSIONERS IN NEW HAMPSHIRE—Continued.

Names.	Acts under which restored.	Remarks.
William Brooks	June 7, 1832	
Abijah Barker	do	
Seth Blake	March 1, 1823	
Moses Brown	do	
Peter Barker	do	
Ensley Brown		
Daniel Cobb		
Clement Corbin	do	
Timothy Clements		
Amos Cogswell		
Jonathan Clark	do	
Aaron Cooley	do	
Abijah Codding	do	
Ebenezer Currier	do	
Joseph Copp	do	
David Campbell		
Jonathan Currier	do	
Corydon Chesley		
Moses Cross	do	
Asa Currier	do	
Jonathan Conant, jr.		
William Cutler		
John Cresey	do	
William Clark	June 7, 1832	
Samuel Cudworth	March 1, 1823	
Thomas Currier, 2d	June 7, 1832	
Joel Carbee	do	
John Colcord		
Daniel Campbell		
Joseph Cheney		
Benjamin Chase		
Nathaniel Clark		
Thomas Cheney	do	
Jonathan Clark, 2d		
Thomas Carr, 2d	March 1, 1823	
Perley Chase	June 7, 1832	
Jesse Campbell	do	
Andrew Cate		
Francis Cobb	do	
Nathaniel Clark, 2d	Invalid roll	Restored to invalid roll under the 3d section of the act of the 1st of May, 1820
John Culver	March 1, 1823	
Ephraim Chamberlin	do	
David Clark	do	
John Cambridge	do	
Thomas Colcord		
Ephraim Doten		
George R. Downing		
Jonas Davis	do	
Thomas Dolloff	do	
Alexander Debell		
Samuel Dale		
John Day	June 7, 1832	
Benaiah Dore	March 1, 1823	
John Davis	do	
Joseph Daniels	do	
Winthrop Davis	June 7, 1832	
Nathaniel Draper		
Joseph Ellis		
Ebenezer Eastman	March 1, 1823	
Thomas Eastman	Invalid	Restored to invalid roll under the 3d section of the act of the 1st of May, 1820

[Doc. No. 127.]

PENSIONERS IN NEW HAMPSHIRE—Continued.

Names.	Acts under which restored.	Remarks.
Nathaniel Evans	June 7, 1832	
Samuel Etkins		
David Ella		
Peter Farnum	March 1, 1823	
John Fox	do	
Moses French	June 7, 1832	
Joseph Felt	March 1, 1823	
Thomas Fuller		
John Fay	do	
Moses Fellows	June 7, 1832	
George Fishley	March 1, 1823	
Benjamin Flint	May 15, 1828	
Samuel Felt	March 1, 1823	
Silas Fox		
Jonathan Ferrin		
Joseph Fellows		
Jabez Felch	do	
John Fields	do	
Jeremiah Fogg	June 7, 1832	
David Flanders	March 1, 1823	
Joseph Fay		
Joshua Farnam	June 7, 1832	
Rufus Fuller	March 1, 1823	
Ebenezer Fielding	do	
Daniel Gookin	do	Relinquished for an increase of his stipend under the act of May 15, 1828.
Jonathan Godfrey	do	
William Gordon		
John Garland	do	
John A. Goss		
Thadeus Gibson	do	
James Gray		
Eleazer Gilson	June 7, 1832	
Amos Gates		
Timothy Gleason	March 1, 1823	
Benjamin Griffen	do	
Ezekiel Gilman		
Samuel Goss		
Mark Green	do	
Solomon Gray		
James Gibson	June 7, 1832	
Joseph Gray	do	
William Gould	March 1, 1823	
James Gilman	June 7, 1832	
Francis Green	do	
Nathaniel Hayes	March 1, 1823	
William Hale	do	
Nathan Hoit	do	
Joseph Homan	do	
Joseph Hull	June 7, 1832	
Joel Holt	do	
Timothy Hall	March 1, 1823	
David Hammond	May 15, 1828	
Amos Heard	March 1, 1823	
Ephraim Ham	do	
Timothy Horsum	do	
Peter Howe	do	
Richard Hall		
Reuben Hall	do	
Daniel Heath		
Joseph Herrick	do	
Sylvanus Hall	do	

[Doc. No. 127.] 17

PENSIONERS IN NEW HAMPSHIRE—Continued.

Names.	Acts under which restored.	Remarks.
John Holmes	March 1, 1823	
Asa Holden	do	
Benjamin Hastings	June 7, 1832	
Thomas Hodge	March 1, 1823	
Benjamin Howard	do	
Moses Harmon	June 7, 1832	
John Hodgkins	do	
Phineas Hamblet	March 1, 1823	
Samuel Howard	do	
Europe Hamlin		
Timothy Holden	June 7, 1832	
Timothy Harvey		
Reuben Hoyt		
Ebenezer Huls	do	
Levi Hutchinson		
Israel Hunt	do	
Thomas Hills	do	
David Hoit	do	
Abner Hogg	do	
Kimber Harvey		
Nathaniel Hayford	March 1, 1823	
Luther Ingalls	do	
David Joslin		
Jonathan Johnson		
Obadiah Jenkins	March 1, 1823	
Benjamin Jewett	May 15, 1823	
Thomas Jamieson	June 7, 1832	
Asa Jones	do	
John Joslin	do	
Samuel Johnson	March 1, 1823	
Moses Knight		
David Kimball	do	
Philip W. Kibby	do	
Reuben Kendall		
Elijah Knight		
Solomon Kittredge	do	
Ephraim Knight		
John Knowlton	do	
Eliphalet Kilburn		
Ichabod Keith	June 7, 1832	
Nathaniel Kelley	March 1, 1823	
Simeon Kemp	do	
Joseph Leach		
Winslow Lakin	do	
Samuel Lear	May 15, 1828	
William Litch		
James Leighton		
Asa Low	March 1, 1823	
Nooah Lewis	Invalid	Also, on roll under the act of the 7th] of June, 1832, in conformity with the act of the 19th February, 1833.
Amos Leavitt	June 7, 1832	
Joseph Little	March 1, 1823	
Jonathan Lougee	do	
Theophilus Levering	do	Relinquished for an increase of his stipend under the act of June 7, 1832.
Benjamin Lamper		
Moses Long	June 7, 1832	
Abiel Lee		
William Lawrence		

2

PENSIONERS IN NEW HAMPSHIRE—Continued.

Names.	Acts under which restored.	Remarks.
Samuel Loverin		
Josiah Lewis		
Samuel Libbee	March 1, 1823	
James Leavitt	do	
Nathaniel Lamb	June 7, 1832	
John Lincoln		
John McIlvain	do	
Ezra Meriam	March 1, 1823	
William McIlvain	June 7, 1832	
Bezeliel Mack	March 1, 1823	
Joseph Mann	do	
Hugh Moore	do	
Phineas Merrill	do	
Thomas Murdough	do	
Nathaniel Martin		
Parker Morgan		
Simeon Mason	do	
Joseph Moor	June 7, 1832	
Joel Miles	March 1, 1823	
Samuel Morse	do	
David Morrill	do	
David Morrison	do	
Joseph Marsh, 1st	do	
Benjamin Morse, 2d	do	
Samuel Morrill	do	
Daniel Moulton		
Joseph Marsh, 2d	June 7, 1832	
Levi Mead		
Joel Megregory	March 1, 1823	
Daniel Marsh		
Jonathan Marsh		
John May	June 7, 1832	
Timothy Metcalf		
James Mullen	March 1, 1823	
Josiah Moor		
John McIntire	June 7, 1832	
Amos Martin	March 1, 1823	
James Nash		
Benjamin Nason	June 7, 1832	
Francis Newton	May 20, 1830	
John Noble		
Philip Nelson	June 7, 1832	
Theophilus Norris	do	
James Orn		
Benjamin Powell	March 1, 1823	
Jonathan Philbrook		
Abner Poland	May 15, 1828	
John Pool		
Richard Perkins	March 1, 1823	
William Parsons		
Henry Parkinson		
David Place		
John Pratt		
John Parker		
David Piper	March 1, 1823	
Moses Perkins	June 7, 1832	
Levi Priest		
James Pelts	March 1, 1823	
Benjamin W. Parker		
Matthew Peck		

PENSIONERS IN NEW HAMPSHIRE—Continued.

Names.	Acts under which restored.	Remarks.
Aaron Parks		
Jonathan Pelts	March 1, 1823	
Benjamin Perkins	June 7, 1832	
William Pritchard	do	
Amariah Partridge		
Joseph Pinneo	March 1, 1823	
Joel Porter	Invalid	Restored to invalid roll under the 3d section of the act of the 1st of May, 1820.
William Parker	June 7, 1832	
Willard Pierce		
Jonathan Parker, 2d		
David Pratt	March 1, 1823	
William Pettingill	June 7, 1832	
Thomas Perkins		
Thomas Ross	March 1, 1823	
Joel Reed	do	
Samuel Rowell	do	
Samuel Remick	Invalid	Again restored under act 1st March, 1823.
John Ricker	March 1, 1823	Relinquished for an increase of his stipend under the act of June 7, 1832.
Joseph Richardson	Invalid	Restored to invalid roll under the 3d section of the act of the 1st of May, 1820.
John Rowe	March 1, 1823	
Otis Robinson	June 7, 1832	
Zachariah Robbins		
George Roberts		
Stephen Richardson		
Joseph Reynolds	June 7, 1832	
Jonathan Russell	March 1, 1823	
Joshua Reed	do	
Benjamin Roberts	do	
Israel Rowell		
Joseph Ripley	do	
Enoch Rowell	do	
Joshua Richardson	do	
James Rider		
Enoch Richardson		
John Roberts	March 1, 1823	
Ezra Read	June 7, 1832	
Stephen Shattuck	March 1, 1823	
James Smith	June 7, 1832	
Jonathan Simonds	do	
Josiah Sanborn	do	
Henry Smith	do	
Isaac Seavy	March 1, 1823	
Joseph Sanborn	June 7, 1832	
Jacob Sinclair		
Francis Smith	March 1, 1823	
Sherburne Sanborn	do	
Jeremy Smith		
John Straw		
Caleb Smart	March 1, 1823	
Elijah Stanton	June 7, 1832	
Abraham T. Sweatt	March 1, 1823	
Edward Smith	do	
James Sanborn		
John Scott	do	
Benjamin Shute	June 7, 1832	
Asa Senter	May 15, 1828	
Amos Smith		

[Doc. No. 127.]

PENSIONERS IN NEW HAMPSHIRE—Continued.

Names.	Acts under which restored.	Remarks.
Joshua Sargent	June 7, 1832	
Aaron Smith	March 1, 1823	
Stephen Smith	do	
Joel Stewart		
Henry Springer	June 7, 1832	
Hezekiah Sawtell	Invalid	Restored to Invalid roll under the 3d section of the act of the 1st of May, 1820.
Ebenezer Scribner		
Charles Stanton	June 7, 1832	
David Sanborn	March 1, 1823	
James Sawyer	June 7, 1832	
Jacob Sullenhein	do	
Calvin Stevens	do	
Shubael Stone		
Moses Straw	March 1, 1823	
Richard Sanborn	do	
Noah Sinclair	Invalid	Restored to Invalid roll under the 3d section of the act of the 1st of May, 1820.
Daniel Swett	June 7, 1832	
David Stratton	May 15, 1828	
Simon C. Stoddard		
David Smiley	March 1, 1823	
Nathan Scarrit		
Jacob Smith, 2d	June 7, 1832	
Samuel Spear		
Josiah Seward		
Stephen Sawyer		
John Shed		
Samuel Steele	do	
Jacob Tilton		
William Taylor		
Benjamin Tarbell	March 1, 1823	
Moses Turner	do	
Benjamin Thatcher	June 7, 1832	
Nicanor Townsley		
Joshua Thompson	May 15, 1828	
Timothy Tilton	March 1, 1823	
Ephraim Tibbetts	do	
Ebenezer Tufts	do	
Christopher Thayer		
Jacob Taylor	June 7, 1832	
William Taggart	Invalid	Restored to Invalid roll under the 3d section of the act of the 1st of May, 1820.
Ralph Thompson	March 1, 1823	Relinquished for an increase of his stipend under the act of June 7, 1832.
Pardon Tabor	June 7, 1832	
Samuel Whiting	March 1, 1823	Relinquished for an increase of his stipend under the act of June, 1832.
Thomas Whittle		
Joseph Whitney		
John Watson	do	
Stephen Webster		
Aaron Willard	do	
Nathaniel Whittemore	do	
Thomas Whipple	do	
Moses Whitaker	June 7, 1832	
Jacob Walden		
Luke Woodbury		
Robert Wilson	do	
Moses Wright	March 1, 1823	

[Doc. No. 127.]   21

PENSIONERS IN NEW HAMPSHIRE—Continued.

Names.	Acts under which restored.	Remarks.
Solomon White	March 1, 1823	Relinquished for an increase of his stipend under the act of the 15th of May, 1828.
William Wheeler	do	
Edward West		
Jonas Whiting		
Eliphalet Wood	do	Relinquished for an increase of his stipend under the act of June 7, 1832.
John Welch	do	
Weymouth Wallace	Invalid	Again restored under act of March 1, 1823.
Leonard Whiting		
Silas Whitney	June 7, 1832	
John White	March 1, 1823	
Stephen Worthen	do	
Stephen White	June 7, 1832	
Benjamin Wheeler	do	
Jacob Wright	March 1, 1823	
Joseph Wheat	May 15, 1828	
James Williams		
Thomas Wilson		
Samuel Willson	March 1, 1823	
Israel Woodbury	June 7, 1832	
Artemas Witt		
Jesse Walker	March 1, 1823	
William Wheeler, 2d	June 7, 1832	
Daniel Wingate		
Elijah Witham		
Alden Washbourne		
Jedediah Weeks		
Abiel Wilson		
Andrew Whitcher	March 1, 1823	
Sutherrick Weston		
James Wood	do	
Jabez Youngman	do	
Thomas Young	do	

[Doc. No. 127.]

PENSIONERS *in Vermont who have been dropped from the pension roll under the act of the 1st of May, 1820, prepared in conformity with the resolution of the House of Representatives of the United States, of the 17th of December, 1835.*

Names.	Acts under which restored.	Remarks.
Jesse Ainger	March 1, 1823	
Edward Allen	May 15, 1828	
John Allen		
Thomas Atwood	June 7, 1832	
Samuel Adams		
John Austin	do.	
James Andrews	March 1, 1823	Relinquished for an increase of his stipend under the act of June 7, 1832.
George Austin		
Isaac Adams		
Jonathan Amidon	June 7, 1832	
Benjamin Andrus		
Philip Alexander	March 1, 1823	
Ezra Allen		
Azor Boughton	May 15, 1828	
Ithiel Barnes	do.	
Jonathan Burnam	June 7, 1832	
Barnabas Barker	March 1, 1823	
Thomas Bogle	do.	
Elijah Baldwin	June 7, 1832	
Ezekiel Beebe	March 1, 1823	
Wolcott Burnham	do.	
Joseph Bowdish		
William Blasdell		
Thomas Betterly	do.	
Gideon Briggs	do.	
Isaac Bump	do.	
John Procter Borres		
John Blackmore		
Barzilla Benjamin	do.	
Friend Beeman	June 7, 1832	
James Britain	do.	
Gideon Buel	do.	
Eleazer Brown	March 1, 1823	
Ebenezer Barry	June 7, 1832	
Samuel Bennett	do.	
Elias Bingham	March 1, 1823	
Zadock Burnam		
Silas Brown		
Abraham Brigham		
Ebenezer Broughton	do.	
Isaac Barrows		
Adonijah Bixby	do.	Relinquished for an increase of his stipend, under the act of June 7, 1832.
Elish Bartlett	June 7, 1832	
Henry Blake	March 1, 1823	
Nathan Barker	do.	
Edmund Beemis		
Thomas Banister		
Elijah Brown	June 7, 1832	
Amos Beckwith		
Daniel Barnum	March 1, 1823	
Solomon Beebe	do.	
Isaac Baldwin	June 7, 1832	
Jesse Bishop	March 1, 1823	
Foard Bears		
Edward Bass		

PENSIONERS IN VERMONT—Continued.

Names.	Acts under which restored.	Remarks.
Benjamin Bugbee		
Thomas Bingham		
Joel Babbitt	March 1, 1823	
Timothy Blake		
James Bishop		
Joel Bolster	June 7, 1832	
Josiah Batchelder	March 1, 1823	
Nathaniel Bosworth	do.	
Peter Benedict		
Joseph Bennet		
John Billings	June 7, 1832	
Solomon Brown	do.	
Phinehas Blood		
Levi Bacon		
Daniel Breck	do.	
Abner Blackmer	March 1, 1823	
Paul Brigham		
Benjamin Bell		
Daniel Burlingame		
Roger Burr		
Elijah Branch	do.	
Dan Barnard	June 7, 1832	
Gideon Brimhall	March 1, 1823	
Asa Boutwell		
Josiah Cutter		
Gideon Curtis	June 7, 1832	
Enoch Carlton	March 1, 1823	
Reuben Church	May 15, 1828	
Joseph Chamberlain		
John Carter	June 7, 1832	
Jonathan Carley	March 1, 1823	
Abel Carpenter	Invalid.	Reinstated as invalid, under the 3d section of the act of May 1, 1820; again restored under the act of March 1, 1823; then relinquished for an increase of his stipend, under the act of June 7, 1832.
Ezekiel Cook		
Benjamin Cheney	March 1, 1832	
John Crane		
Peter Clays	May 15, 1828	
Isaac Church	March 1, 1823	
Royal Crowley	June 7, 1832	
Eliphalet Carpenter	do.	
Comfort Chaffee		
Samuel Currier		
Nathaniel Chaney		
Emerson Corliss	March 1, 1823	
John Chadwick		
Squire Cleveland	June 7, 1832	
Jonas Cutting	March 1, 1823	
Ebenezer Chamberlin	do.	
Abel Conant	June 7, 1832	
Leander Chamberlin		
James Crane	do.	
Elias Carpenter	do.	
Stephen Chase		
John Cobb	March 1, 1823	
Joseph Cummins	do.	
James Campbell, 2d	do.	
Nathaniel Chaffee		
John Carpenter	June 7, 1832	
John Cummings	May 15, 1828	

[Doc. No. 127.]

PENSIONERS IN VERMONT—Continued.

Names.	Acts under which restored.	Remarks.
Samuel Clapp		
Anthony Collamer		
Isaac Cady	March 1, 1823	
Jonathan Cadwell		
Asa Clark		
Paul Clark	May 15, 1828	
Nathaniel Cole		
Isaac Cutler	March 1, 1823	
Archibald Cook		
Swift Chamberlain		
Julius Colton		
Isaac Chace	June 7, 1832	
Ebenezer Chace		
Richard Carlton		
Solomon Cleavland		
Abel Camp	do.	
Hull Curtis	do.	
Nathaniel Cutter	March 1, 1823	
Daniel Champin	June 7, 1832	
James Chittenden	do.	
Henry Chamberlin	March 1, 1823	
David Carlton	June 7, 1832	
Asa Coburn	do.	
Simeon Curtis	March 1, 1823	
Lemuel Clark	do.	
Amos Dennison		
Frederick Dickerman	do.	
James L. Dean	June 7, 1832	
Peter Danforth		
Jared Dixon	March 1, 1823	
Alexander Durand	do.	
Jerathmeel Doty	do.	Reinstated as invalid, under the 3d section of the act of May 1, 1820; restored under the act of March 1, 1823.
Francis Donita	June 7, 1832	
Ephraim Dutton	March 1, 1823	
Ebenezer Drake		
Joseph Demick		
Gershom Dunham	June 7, 1832	
Joseph Doubleday		
Jonathan Dix		
John Dexter	do.	
John Dudley	March 1, 1823	
Daniel Davison, jr.		
Amos Dwinell	June 7, 1832	
Josiah Dana		
Samuel Davis	March 1, 1823	
Jonathan Deming	May 15, 1828	
Caleb Eddy		
Jonathan Emmons	March 1, 1823	
Gamaliel Ellis	do.	
Ralph Ellenwood	June 7, 1832	
Josiah Eastman	March 1, 1823	
Reuben Evarts	June 7, 1832	
Samuel Edson		
Seth Eddy		
Ariel Egerton	do.	
Samuel Eastman		
Benjamin Everest	March 1, 1823	
Amaza Fuller	do.	
Ebenezer Flagg		
James Fosdick	do.	

[Doc. No. 127.]   25

PENSIONERS IN VERMONT—Continued.

Names.	Acts under which restored	Remarks.
Joseph Frost		
John Frizzle	June 7, 1832	
Timothy Fisher	March 1, 1823	
Asa Fay		
William Flagg	June 7, 1832	
Jonathan French	March 1, 1823	
Jonathan Farnsworth	June 7, 1832	
Thomas Fay		
Bazalel Farnham		
John Fendley		
Moses Fay		
Abel Fling	do.	
Daniel Fuller	do.	
Samuel Freeman	May 15, 1828	
Thomas Fuller		
Ephraim Fuller		
Elisha A. Fowler	June 7, 1832	
Stephen Fisk	do.	
Ezekiel Fullington	do.	
Ezekiel Flanders	do.	
Gamaliel Gerald		
John Gates	June 7, 1832	
Asa Gage	March 1, 1823	
Jacob Gould		
William Gill	March 1, 1823	
Bethuel Goodrich, sen.	do.	
Jesse Child	June 7, 1832	
Azariah Grant		
Michael George	March 1, 1823	
Obadiah Gill	do.	
Silas Gorham	do.	
Samuel Gordon	do.	
Calvin Goodno, alias, Goodenough	do.	
Isaac Glinney	do.	
Benjamin George	do.	
Jonas Gates	do.	
Joshua Geary	do.	
Andrew Grimes	do.	
Samuel Gates	June 7, 1832	
John Gould	March 1, 1823	
Edmund Grundy		
Alvin Goodall	do.	
Solomon Gilson	do.	
Moses Haskell	do.	
Cyrus Hill	do.	
Samuel Houghton		
Daniel Harris	do.	
Aaron Hitchcock		
William Harris		
William Hunt		
Joseph Hixon		
Ephraim Holden	June 7, 1832	
John Hasey	March 1, 1823	
Benjamin Hardy	do.	
Joseph Howe		
William Harris, 2d		
Ephraim Holridge	do.	
Seth Hubbell	do.	
Richard Hill		
Jonathan Hunter	do.	
John Hollenbeck, or Holomback		

[Doc. No. 127.]

PENSIONERS IN VERMONT—Continued.

Names.	Acts under which restored.	Remarks.
Hiram Huntington	June 7, 1832	
Reuben Holland		
James Hyde	May 15, 1828	
Daniel Hunt		
Enoch Hoyt	March 1, 1823	
Abner Hubbard	do.	
Thomas Haseltine	May 15, 1828	
James Hooker	do.	
Joseph House		
Elisha Hurlbut		
Amos Holbrook	March 1, 1823	
Jacob Haskell	June 7, 1832	
Robert Holley	do.	
Jonas Haynes	do.	
Ichabod Higgins	March 1, 1823	
Josiah Hubbard	June 7, 1832	
David Hibbard	do.	
Samuel Hill	March 1, 1823	
Adam Howard	une 7, 1832	
Archibald Harvey		
Timothy Hall	do.	
Asahel Hills		
Jonas Hubbard	May 15, 1828	
Jehiel Hull		
Seth Hoyt		
Luke Hitchcock	June 7, 1832	He could not take the oath prescribed by the act of May 1, 1820, not being a citizen of the United States.
John Hutchinson	do.	
Jonathan Jackson		
Ephraim Jackson	March 1, 1823	
William Johnston		
William Jennison	June 7, 1832	
William Isham	May 15, 1828	
Enoch Jenkins	do.	
Stephen Jennings		
Oliver Jones	March 1, 1823	
James Johnson	do.	
Stephen Jones	June 7, 1832	
Benjamin Joy	March 1, 1823	
Ichabod King	do.	
William Kinney		
Henry Keeler	do.	
John Keyes		
James Kilborn	do.	
Amos Kimball	do.	
Josiah Knight		
Phineas Kellog	June 7, 1832	
Martin Kellog	do.	
Eleazer Knap		
John Keison	do.	
Richard Kimball		
Thomas Keyes	March 1, 1823	
Samuel Lovering		
Joshua Lawrence		
Joseph Lamb	do.	
Daniel Lincoln	do.	
Theophilus Larabe		
Eli Lewis	June 7, 1832	
William Lewis	March 1, 1823	
John Lynch	do.	
Thomas Leland	do.	

PENSIONERS IN VERMONT—Continued.

Names.	Acts under which restored.	Remarks.
Benjamin Lynde	March 1, 1823	
Elisha Lincoln	do.	
Benjamin Lilley		
John Lines	May 15, 1828	
Cornelius Lynde	June 7, 1832	
William Larabe	March 1, 1823	
Moses Lurvey	do.	
Moses Leach	do.	
Augustus Lavoke, Levaque, or Levague		
William Lord	do.	
Levi Lufkin	do.	
Samuel McConnel		
Noah Merritt	June 7, 1832	
Samuel Miller	do.	
Samuel Moore	March 1, 1823	
John Moores	do.	
Peter Martin		
Thomas May		
Samuel Myrick	May 15, 1828	
Robert Miller		
Thomas McNeil		
Jacob McLean		
William McAlister		
Silas McWithey	March 1, 1823	
Benjamin Metcalf	do.	
James Magar		
Sylvanus Mattoon	do.	
Jesse Marks		
Reuben Martin	June 7, 1832	
Thomas McKeith		
Rufus Moore	do.	
Samuel Mills	do.	
Benjamin Mack		
John Moore	March 1, 1823	
Stephen Murray	June 7, 1832	
Ashbel Mason	March 1, 1823	
Noah Merrill		
James Martin		
John Martin		
Samuel Martin	do.	
Mansfield Nichols		
Humphrey Nichols	do.	
Joseph Norton	June 7, 1832	
David Nichols	do.	
Gideon Newton		
Israel Newton		
Jabez Newland	do.	
Reverius Newell	March 1, 1823	
Eliada Orton		
William Orcutt	March 1, 1823	
Thomas Osgood	May 15, 1828	
Jonathan Orms	June 7, 1832	
Eleazer Owen	do.	
Amos Prouty	do.	
James Parley	do.	
Samuel Parker	do.	
Joel W. Perham	March 1, 1823	
William Pratt	do.	
Nehemiah Philips	May 15, 1828	
Elisha Pulford	do.	
Pelatiah Philips	March 1, 1823	

PENSIONERS IN VERMONT—Continued.

Names.	Acts under which restored.	Remarks.
Samuel Peirce		
Jonathan Powers	June 7, 1832	
Benjamin Packard		
Kiles Paul		
Burphy Prouty	March 1, 1823	
Samuel Petty	do.	
Matthew Pratt		
Abisha Packard	June 7, 1832	
Abner Perry	March 1, 1823	
Francis Perkins	do.	
Samuel Peek		
Benjamin Pierce		
Amos Page		
Charles Paine	do.	
Abner Perkins		
Abel Peirce, 2d		
Benjamin Preston	do.	
Daniel Perkins		
William Powell		
Thomas Page	June 7, 1832	
Parker Page	do.	
Nathan Page		
Isaac Pinney	May 31, 1830	Special act.
David Pierce		
Amos Page	June 7, 1832	
Andrew Parsons		
Francis Phelps	do.	
Joshua Philips	March 1, 1823	
Asahel Powers		
Richard Pearse	June 7, 1832	
Silas Pratt		
Aaron Parker		
Silas Perry		
Simeon Post		
Joseph Powers		
Samuel Phelps	March 1, 1823	
Philemon Parker	do.	
Asa Richardson, alias Fidelio Richardson		
John Rumsay	May 15, 1828	
Samuel Ranger	March 1, 1823	
Joseph Randall		
Luke Roberts	do.	
Isaac Rice		
Joseph Raymond		
Zephaniah Ross	May 20, 1830	
Peter Reynolds	June 7, 1832	
James Robinson	March 1, 1823	
John Riddall	June 7, 1832	
Humphrey Richardson	March 1, 1823	
Moses Rowell		
Elijah Roice	June 7, 1832	
David Russell	do.	
Cornelius Russell		
David Rusco	March 1, 1823	
Eleazer Robinson		
Jonathan Reynolds		
Stephen Russell	June 7, 1832	
Joseph Randall, 2d	do.	
Rufus Root	March 1, 1823	
Isaac Rexford		
Simeon Russell, 2d		

PENSIONERS IN VERMONT—Continued.

Names.	Acts under which restored.	Remarks.
Jonathan Stevens	March 1, 1823	Relinquished for an increase of his stipend under the act of 7th June, 1832.
Ethiel Scott	do.	
Roger Smith	do.	
Silas Simonds	do.	
Solomon Smith	June 7, 1832	
Stephen Sweetzer		
Jonathan Sheppard	do.	
Thomas Stickney	March 1, 1823	
Benjamin B. Searl	June 7, 1832	
John Smith, 2d	do.	
Benjamin Smith		
Jonathan Sawyer	March 1, 1823	
Jedediah Smith	May 15, 1828	
Peter Stevens		
William Spooner	March 1, 1823	
Nathan Smith	do.	
Calvin Seaver	June 7, 1832	
Benjamin Stevens, alias Leach		
David Shipherd	do.	
Ebenezer Summers	do.	
Jonathan Stoddard		
Josiah Smith		
James Shaw	do.	
Zephaniah Sheoardson		
Conant Sawyer	March 1, 1823	
Zadock Steele	June 7, 1832	
Joseph Stannard		
Josiah Sawyer		
Samuel Spaulding	do.	
William Strobridge	do.	
William Seymour	do.	
Thomas Scott	March 1, 1823	
Hezekiah Tinkhum	May 15, 1828	
Hezekiah Tuttle	March 1, 1823	
Simon Tubbs		
Samuel Torry	May 15, 1828	
Solomon Tracy		
Isaac Tillotson	March 1, 1823	
Jeremiah Tyler	June 7, 1832	
Asa Thatcher	March 1, 1823	
David Town	do.	
Thomas Thompson		
Thomas Todd	June 7, 1832	
Gideon Tabor		
Stephen Trowbridge	May 15, 1828	
Samuel Taylor		
James Taylor	June 7, 1832	
Isaac Thayer	do.	
Joseph Taggart	do.	
Jerijah Thayer	March 1, 1823	
Jacob Taylor	do.	
Abel Titus	June 7, 1832	
George Townsend		
David Thomas		
James Tyler	do.	
Abel Titus	do.	
Stephen Terrill	March 1, 1823	
Jonathan Taylor	do.	
Nathaniel B. Torry		
Loring Thompson	do.	
Joseph Underwood		

[Doc. No. 127.]

PENSIONERS IN VERMONT—Continued.

Names.	Acts under which restored.	Remarks.
James Upham	March 1, 1823	
John Underwood	do.	
Samuel Viall	do.	
Noah Villars		
John Vinton		
Samuel White	Invalid	Reinstated on invalid roll under the 3d section of the act of 1st May, 1820.
Jabez Ward		
James Willis		
Edward West	June 7, 1832	
Benjamin Wocster	do.	
William White	do.	
John Williams, 2d		
Timothy Willmot		
Joseph Williams		
Isaac Webster	Invalid	Reinstated on invalid roll under the 3d section of the act of 1st May, 1820.
Benjamin Walker		
Asahel Wright	May 15, 1828	
John Wiman	March 1, 1823	
Lot Woodbury	do.	
Edward Wade	May 15. 1828	
William Waterman	June 7, 1832	
Moses Weld	May 20, 1830	
Archibald White		
Daniel Woods	March 1, 1823	
James Whelpley	do.	
Asa Wheeler		
Frederick Ware	do.	
Badwell Watkins		
Jesse Ward	June 7, 1832	
Moses Wheeler		
William Whitman	March 1, 1823	
Ephraim Whitcomb		
Calvin Weld		
George Williamson		
Nathan White		
Timothy Woodford		
Jabez Wight	do.	
Henry Wilson	do.	
Gershom York	do.	

[Doc. No. 127.] 31

PENSIONERS in Massachusetts who have been dropped from the pension roll under the act of 1st of May, 1820; prepared in conformity with the resolution of the House of Representatives of the United States of the 17th of December, 1835.

Names.	Acts under which restored.	Remarks.
John Andrews		
John Annabel	March 1, 1823	
Robert Annabel	do.	
Caleb Albee	June 7, 1832	
Abner Allen	do.	
Asa Albee	do.	
Luther Adkins	do.	
Noah Allen		
David Anderson	do.	
John Allen		
Ansell Adams	March 1, 1823	
Elijah Allen	do.	
Seth Allen	June 7, 1832	
Thomas Andros	do.	
Nathaniel Allen	March 1, 1823	
Nathaniel Avery	June 7, 1832	
Nathaniel Allen, 2d		
Noah Ashley	do.	
Miles Avery	May 15, 1828	
Thomas Avery	Invalid	Restored as invalid under the 3d section of the act of 1st of May, 1820.
Stephen Allen		
Jonathan Avery	March 1, 1823	
John Adams	May 15, 1828	
Nehemiah Abbott	June 7, 1832	
Ebenezer Burrill		
Rufus Burnham	March 1, 1823	
Frederick Breed		
William Bancroft	do.	
Josiah Bowers	June 7, 1832	
Elisha Brewster	May 15, 1828	
Jacob Bates	March 1, 1823	
Daniel Bartlett		
Jonas Bemis, 1st	May 15, 1828	
Jesse Bemis	June 7, 1832	
Isaac Briant	do.	
Samuel Babbit		
Eleazar Ball		
Abial Burgess	March 1, 1823	
Samuel Bacon	June 7, 1832	
David Boyce	do.	
Alden Burrill	March 1, 1823	
Jonas Bayley		
John Ball	do.	
Patrick Bryant	June 7, 1832	
Dimon Bradley	- -	In this case the pensioner never exhibited a schedule of his property; but his pension was stopped because the department was informed that he was not in needy circumstances.
John Brett	do.	
Jonas Bemis, 2d		
Andrew Bigelow	March 1, 1823.	
Samuel Beach	do.	
Thomas Boyden		
Aaron Bolton	June 7, 1832	
Ebenezer Bowtelle	do.	
William Buck	do.	

PENSIONERS IN MASSACHUSETTS—Continued.

Names.	Acts under which restored.	Remarks.
Elisha Blandin	March 1, 1823	
David Bradley	May 15, 1828	
Jonathan Ball, 2d		
Israel Bullock		
Jacob Briggs, jr.	March 1, 1823	
Caleb Blackslee	May 15, 1828	
Daniel Brown		
John Burridge		
John Bacon		
Joseph Buel	June 7, 1832	
Abel Benson	March 1, 1823	
Samuel Belcher	June 7, 1832	
Joseph Bowtelle	March 1, 1823	
Simeon Blanchard	do.	
Elijah Borden	do.	
Josiah Bemis		
Joseph Bates		
Luther Bailey		
Robert Bragg		
Job Brocklebank		
Thomas Barnes		
William Benjamin		
Joseph Burbeck		
James Bancroft	do.	
Sherajashub Bowen		
Joseph Bonney	June 7, 1832	
Leonard Briggs	March 1, 1823	
Samuel Bates	June 7, 1832	
Newman Bishop	do.	
Jonathan Barrett	do.	
John Bullard		
David Bradford	March 1, 1823	
John Bixby		
John Butler		
Eleazar Bates		
William Bogle	June 7, 1832	
Jonathan Bancroft	March 1, 1823	
Enoch Baldwin		
Jonathan Bates, 2d		
Sylvanus Brimhall	June 7, 1832	
Joshua Brewster	do.	
Peter Brow	March 1, 1823	
Warren Brigham	June 7, 1832	
Jeremiah Burnham		
Benjamin Bisby	do.	
Asa Bumpus	March 1, 1823	
Elisha Bosworth	June 7, 1832	
Roger Benjamin	do.	
John Bolton		
Timothy Bellows		
Hezekiah Bush	do.	
Charles Burnham	March 1, 1823	
William Badger		
Daniel Brown		
Samuel Buffington	May 15, 1828	
William Blanchard	June , 1832	
William Bartlett	do.	
Joseph Burnell		
John Bailey	March 1, 1823	
William Brewster		
Amos Boardman		
Jacob Brown	June 7, 1832	

PENSIONERS IN MASSACHUSETTS—Continued.

Names.	Acts under which restored.	Remarks.
Abner Blanchard	June 7, 1832	
Edmund Blood	do.	
Amos Brown		
Henry Brigham		
Jabez Brooks	do.	
John Howe Boardman	do.	
Abiezer Briggs	do.	
Ebenezer Bacon		
John Baker	March 1, 1823	
Isaac Bowen Barker	June 7, 1832	
Joseph Bond	do.	
Abijah Chever	May 15, 1828	
Jonathan Crosby		
James Capron	June 7, 1832	
James Conant	March 1, 1823	
Samuel Cole	June 7, 1832	
Aaron Crumbie		
George Coffin	do.	
William Crowningshield		
John Chandler		
Michael Carlton		
David Clark	March 1, 1823	
Jacob Clarke	June 7, 1832	
Joseph Clarke	May 15, 1828	
Alpheus Colton		
Lemuel Coffin	March 1, 1823	
Robert Cottle	do.	
George Cooley		
Eliakim Clapp		
Isaac Chapin	June 7, 1832	
John Coats		
Jacob Cole	do.	
James Cole		
Josiah Cushman	do.	
Asa Chase	do.	
Peter Crane		
Daniel Coburn	March 1, 1823	
Luther Conant	do.	
Azariah Cooley		
John Call		
Earl Cutting	June 7, 1832	
Beriah Clark		
Adams Chapin	do.	
Jonathan Cressey		
Joseph Cheever	March 1, 1823	
Joseph Chandler	June 7, 1832	
Noah Cook		
James Cassell	do.	
James Claridge		
Ebenezer Clark, 1st		
Ebenezer Winter Calef		
Ebenezer Capen		
Abijah Child		
Simeon Cole	do.	
George Cushman	March 1, 1823	
Asa Clark	June 7, 1832	
Moses Craig	do.	
Gideon Clark		
Simeon Crosman		
Caleb Church		
Joseph Carey	do.	
Ephraim Cushman	March 1, 1823	

PENSIONERS IN MASSACHUSETTS—Continued.

Names.	Acts under which restored.	Remarks.
Ebenezer Covel	March 1, 1823	
Benjamin Crowingshield	June 7, 1832	
James Cooper		
James Croswell		
Selden Crooker		
William Cornish	do.	
Daniel Cone	do.	
Benjamin Croswell		
Joseph Conner		
John Chase		
Aaron Carey		
Isaac Coit	do.	
John Clark		
Nathan Cory		
Gideon Coggeshall		
Oliver Comee	do.	
Timothy Childs		
Ezra Carpenter	do.	
William S. Cruttenden	do.	
Thomas Church		
Enoch Chase		
William Cushing	Invalid	Inscribed as invalid under the 3d section of the act of 1st May, 1820.
Uriah Church		
Andrew Cole	June 7, 1832	
Francis Carey	March 1, 1823	
John Coolidge		
Dwilly Clapp		
Moses Collins	June 7, 1832	
Thomas Clark		
John Clark	do.	
Philip Curtis	do.	
Ebenezer Clark, 2d	March 1, 1823	
Benjamin Cressey	do.	
Thomas Davis	June 7, 1832	
Palfrey Downing	May 15, 1828	
Samuel Dodge	March 1, 1823	
William Davenport		
Bennett Davis	do.	
Artemas Dryden	June 7, 1832	
Israel Dodge		
Joshua Danforth	May 15, 1828	
Joseph Dwelley	June 7, 1832	
John Davis		
Jonathan Deacons		
Amariah Daniels		
Solomon Dwinel		
George Dunham		
Solomon Davie		
Samuel Daggett	March 1, 1823	
James Davenport		
Nathan Dewing	do.	
Jeremiah Driscoll		
John Dobson		
John Daniels	June 7, 1832	
John Dewing	do.	
Jesse Delano	March 1, 1823	
Isaac Dennison	June 7, 1832	
Myles Doran		
Ebenezer Dunbar		
Thomas Dean		
Samuel Dorr	May 15, 1828	

PENSIONERS IN MASSACHUSETTS—Continued.

Names.	Acts under which restored.	Remarks.
Elisha Dexter	June 7, 1832	
Lemuel Dean	do.	
William Drake	do.	
William Dickson	do.	
Robert Day		
Joseph Doubleday	do.	
William Draper	March 1, 1823	
Josiah Dunbar	do.	
Jesiah Davis	do.	
Peter Dickerman		
Isaac Dade		
James Derumple	June 7, 1832	
Zelek Darling	do.	
Elijah Daggett	March 1, 1823	
Ephraim Emerton		
Joseph Eveleth	June 7, 1832	
John Ellingwood	March 1, 1823	
William Ellingwood	June 7, 1832	
Joseph Eaton	do.	
Benjamin Emerson		
Ebenezer Eddy	May 15, 1828	
Charles Emes	March 1, 1832	
John Edwards Ely		
John Emerson	June 7, 1832	
Michael Eagles	March 1, 1823	
John Edmonds	June 7, 1832	
Pearson Eaton		
Aaron Eveleth	do.	
Zebulon Elwell		
William Evans	do.	
Ebenezer Edson		
Abraham Edwards		
Seth Edson	do.	
Samuel Eddy	do.	
Joshua Eddy	do.	
Noah Eager		
Nehemiah Emerson	May 15, 1828	
Nehemiah Eastbrook		
James Emerson	March 1, 1823	
Loved Eddy		
Levi Fay	June 7, 1832	
Haskell Freeman		
John Fessenden	May 15, 1828	
Leonard Foster	March 1, 1823	
Nathaniel Friend	June 7, 1832	
David Foster		
Joseph Felt	March 1, 1823	
Jonathan Flagg	June 7, 1832	
Curtis Fowle		
John Foster	March 1, 1823	
Joseph Foster	June 7, 1832	
Joshua Frye		
Benjamin Felton		
James Freeman	March 1, 1823	
William Faris	June 7, 1832	
Thomas Fay	March 1, 1823	
Joseph Farwell	June 7, 1832	
Zedekiah Fisk	do.	
Aaron Fisher	do.	
John Fobes	do.	
Asaph Faxon		
Thadeus Fitch		

PENSIONERS IN MASSACHUSETTS—Continued.

Names.	Acts under which restored.	Remarks.
Joshua French	June 7, 1832	
Israel Fisher	March 1, 1823	
Jesse Fowler		
David Fiske		
Nathaniel French, 2d	do	
Thomas Freeman		
Jonathan Fairbanks	do	
John Frink		
Asher Freeman		
Josiah Fuller		
Abraham Foster		
Nathan Fuller		
Thomas Florence		
Josiah Fuller, 2d	June 7, 1832	
Ezekiel Fuller	do	
Samuel Fales	March 1, 1823	
Joshua Fletcher	June 7, 1832	
John Fowle		
Joseph Freeland	do	
Calvin Fillebrown		
Jason Fisher		
Prince Ford	do	
William Fairbank	do	
James Frost		
George Fairbank		
Joseph Fisk	May 15, 1828	
Isaac Fish	March 1, 1823	
Edward Fobes		
Caleb Faxon		
Benjamin Farnum	Invalid	Inscribed as invalid under 3d section of the act of 1st of May, 1820.
Benjamin Franklin	June 7, 1832	
Samuel Goodrich		
Gideon Graves	May 15, 1828	
Jonathan Gale	March 1, 1823	
John Greene		
Thadeus Gilbert	do	
George Gorham	do	
Jonah Gross		
William Greenleaf	do	Relinquished for an increase of his stipend under act of May 15, 1828.
Daniel Gray	June 7, 1832	
Jonas Gilbert	do	
Joel Gilbert	do	
Aaron Greenwood		
Thomas Greenwood		
Noah Goodrich		
Zacheus Goldsmith	March 1, 1823	
Joseph Guild	May 15, 1828	
Abner Graves		
Cabarabzarman Gould	March 1, 1823	
Samuel Gould, 1st	June 7, 1832	
John George		
Robert Gaylord		
Barnabas Griffith		
David Grover		
Elisha Grose	May 15, 1828	
Levi Gurney	March 1, 1823	
Thomas Gray		
George Gorham	do	
Joel Grout	June 7, 1832	
Cæsar Godfrey		

[Doc. No. 127.]. 37

PENSIONERS IN MASSACHUSETTS—Continued.

Names.	Acts under which restored.	Remarks.
Selah Graves		
Joshua Gott	June 7, 1832	
John Gelat	do	
Richard Gundeway		
Isaac Green	do	
Abraham Gould	March 1, 1832	
Levi Graves	do	
William Green	June 7, 1832	
Isaac Goodenow	March 1, 1823	
William Gordon	May 15, 1828	
Peter Gibson	June 7, 1832	
Justin Granger		
Thomas Gay	March 1, 1823	
Ebenezer Hart	May 15, 1828	
Henry Hallowell	March 1, 1823	
William Hill		
Eliphalet Holman	June 7, 1832	
William Hilbert	March 1, 1823	
Nathaniel Hitchings	do	
John Hood	do	
Nathaniel Houghton	do	
Lemuel Herrington	June 7, 1832	
Ichabod Hickock		
John Hosley		
Daniel Harris	do	
Josiah Hinshaw, or Hincher		
Lemuel Healy	do	
Samuel Hudson		
Jonathan Hunt	do	
Noah Hunt	March 1, 1823	
Moses Hoyt		
Jonathan Harris		
Joab Holland		
Reuben Haynes	June 7, 1832	
Benjamin Hobbs, 1st	March 1, 1823	
Agrippa Hull	May 15, 1828	
Richard Hood	March 1, 1823	
Gershom Harwood		
David Hearsey		
Theophilus Hastings	do	
Asa Hebard	do	
Jacob Hayden		
Andrew Howard	do	
Eliakim Hamilton	June 7, 1832	
Noah Harrod		
Richard Hines		
Jeffry Hemenway		
Oliver Harris	do	
Enoch Horton	March 1, 1823	
William Hayden		
William Hearsey	do	
Levi Hodge		
Ezekiel Howard		
Gershom Hyde	June 7, 1832	
David Holmes		
Richard Herrick	March 1, 1823	
David How		
Martin Herrick		
David Hoyt		
Zadock Howe		
Lot Hunt		

PENSIONERS IN MASSACHUSETTS—Continued.

Names.	Acts under which restored.	Remarks.
Azor Howe	March 1, 1823	
William Hyland	June 7, 1832	
Samuel Hyland	March 1, 1823	
Ezra Hayden		
Nathan Hicks	June 7, 1832	
David Holbrook	March 1, 1823	Relinquished for an increase of his stipend under the act of May 15, 1828.
Dominicus Hovey		
John Hopkins	do	
Josiah Hathaway		
John Haven		
Ziba Hayden		
Daniel Hayden		
Leonard Hill		
Joshua Haskins	June 7, 1832	
Moses Hancock		
Benjamin Henderson	do	
Jacob Haskin		
Philip Haskell	do	
Aaron Hall	do	
Darius Holbrook	do	
Experience Hammond		
Alexander Hunter		
William Hayden, 2d	do	
Aaron Hayes	do	
Joseph Hodgkins		
Michael Henry		
Nathaniel Holmes	do	
Jonathan Hildrith		
Josiah Hall	do	
James Hayes		
Asa Hill		
Silas Hartshorn		
Elisha Hall		
John Hurley		
Braddock Hoar		
Noah Hobart	do	
Elijah Hazeltine		
Titus Hubbard	do	
John Howard	do	
Edward Houghton		
Laban Hall	March 1, 1823	
Peter Hearsey	do	
Oliver Harris, 2d	do	
Preserved Hoskins	June 7, 1832	
John Hoppin	March 1, 1823	
David Houston		
Thomas Hurd	June 7, 1832	
Benjamin Howes	do	
Jeremiah Hartshorne	do	
Joshua Harding	March 1, 1823	
Edward Johnson		
James Ingalls		
Isaiah Ilsley	do	
Abel Jones	do	
Benjamin Johnson		
David Johnson	June 7, 1832	
David Jewett	May 15, 1828	
Samuel P. Jones		
John Jepherson	June 7, 1832	
Ebenezer Jackson		
John Johnson	March 1, 1823	

[Doc. No. 127.] 89

PENSIONERS IN MASSACHUSETTS—Continued.

Names.	Acts under which restored.	Remarks.
Elisha Johnson	June 7, 1832	
Nathaniel Johnston, 1st		
Consider Jones		
Nathan Ide	March 1, 1823	
Daniel Jackson	May 15, 1828	
Nathan Jaques		
Nathan Johnson		
Francis Josselyn	March 1, 1823	
Simpson Jones		
Jesse Jordon		
Richard Johnson	June 7, 1832	
Thomas Jones	March 1, 1823	
William Jones		
Asa Jonson		
Oliver Judd	June 7, 1832	
John Jepson		
Zadock Ingell	do	
Oliver Jewett		
Seth Johnson		
Joseph Jepson	do	
Nathaniel Knight	do	
Jabez Keep		
Thomas Kendall	do	
Richard Kimball		
Joseph Kemp		
Boice Kimball		
Edward Kilton	March 1, 1823	
Abijah Knapp	do	
Aaron Kingsbury		
Stephen King		
John Kidder	do	
Jonathan Knowlton	June 7, 1832	
William Kimball		
Abraham Knowlton		
Maurice Kelly		
Samuel Kimball		
William Knight	do	
Jabez Kirkland, alias Kirtland	do	
William Kelham	March 1, 1823	
Eliphalet King		
David Legg, 2d	March 1, 1823	
David Legg, 1st	June 7, 1832	
Ebenezer Lovett		
Isaac Lovejoy		
John Lamb		
Josiah Lawrence	do	
Levi Lesure		
Elihu Lyman		
William Lewis		
Daniel Lamb		
Jacob Leonard		
Barnabas Lathrop	do	
Josiah Lee	March 1, 1823	
Solomon Lee	do	
Joseph Lee		
Benjamin Larned		
Isaac Lee	do	
Joseph Lilley		
Rowland Luce	do	
Rufus Lincoln	do	Relinquished for an increase of his stipen under the act of May 15 1828
David Lord		

[Doc. No. 127.]

PENSIONERS IN MASSACHUSETTS—Continued.

Names.	Acts under which restored.	Remarks.
Daniel Learned		
Nathaniel Long		
Jesse Lovejoy		
Jonathan Lombard	March 1, 1823	
Ziba Leonard	June 7, 1832	
Elkenah Linnell	March 1, 1823	
Josiah Linnell		
Nathan Lazell	June 7, 1832	
John Lincoln		
Ezekiel Leach		
Aaron Lumbard		
Timothy Lunt		
Thomas Laurence		
John Merritt		
John Melcoy	March 1, 1823	
Stephen Mitchell		
Mark Morse	do	
Ebenezer Morse	June 7, 1832	
William Moore		
James Melvin	May 15, 1828	
Bannister Maynard		
Benjamin Morse	do	
Amos Munroe		
Obadiah Morse		
Enos Marsh	June 7, 1832	
David Marston		
James Martin		
Tilly Mead	March 1, 1823	
Levi May	do	
Eliphaz Mitchell		
Reuben Moore	June 7, 1832	
Edward Masters		
Job Miller	do	
Robert Milton		
Robert Mullet		
Chester Morse		
William Mills	March 1, 1823	
Abraham Morrison		
Jonathan Maynard	May 15, 1828	
Joel Morse		
Amos Morse	March 1, 1823	
William Mathews, 2d		
Jonathan Merry		
Samuel Morey	do	
Phinehas Manning	May 15, 1828	
Thomas Mallord	March 1, 1823	
John McDaniel or McDonough		
Samuel G. Morton		
Joseph Morse	June 7, 1832	
Israel Manning		
John Manning, 2d		
John Mears		
Freeburn Mahen		
Comfort Martin		
Duty Marsh		
Dudly Maxfield	do	
Joseph Nye		
Aaron Nurse		
John Norton	March 1, 1823	
Samuel Newell	June 7, 1832	
Thomas Nichols	March 1, 1823	
Henry Norwell	June 7, 1832	

[Doc. No. 127.]   41

PENSIONERS IN MASSACHUSETTS—Continued.

Names.	Acts under which restored.	Remarks.
Job Nash	June 7, 1832	
Jonathan Nichols		
James Nourse	Invalid	Restored as invalid under 3d section of act of May 1, 1820, subsequently restored under act of March 1, 1823.
Charles Newcomb		
John Nutting	March 1, 1823	
Joseph Newell		
Nathan Newman	June 7, 1832	
Daniel Newhall	do	
Ebenezer Nutting		
Samuel Nightingale		
Paul Newton	do	
Samuel Nash	do	
Thomas Nixon	do	
Daniel Nutting	Invalid	Inscribed on invalid roll under 3d section of act of May 1, 1820; also, on roll under act of June 7, 1832.
William Onthank		
Richard Ober		
Samuel Orcutt	June 7, 1832	
Russel Oliver		
Isaac Orgin	March 1, 1823	
Ephraim Orcutt	do	
John Oldham	do	
John Osborn, 2d	June 7, 1832	
Samuel Osgood		
Micah Orcutt	do	
Eleazer Owen	do	
Ebenezer Parsons	do	
John Perkins	do	
Robert Parker		
Amos Pierce	do	
Eli Prouty		
Joseph Peagan		
Joseph Pierce, 1st	March 1, 1823	
James Patch	June 7, 1832	
William Pecker		
Francis Peabody	March 1, 1823	
John Picket		
Joel Pratt	do	Relinquished for an increase of his stipend under the act of May 15, 1828.
Joseph Pierce, 2d	June 7, 1832	
Luther Parmenter	do	
Solomon Parsons	Invalid	Inscribed as invalid under the 3d section of the act of May 1, 1820.
Abel Partridge		
Eldad Parsons		
Sylvanus Parsons		
Nathan Putnam		
William Parker, 2d		
Benjamin Pettingell	June 7, 1832	
David Pike	do	
James Peck		
Joshua Packard		
Ephraim Parminter		
Jonathan Parkhurst	March 1, 1823	
Samson Presho		
Samuel Punchard		
Amos Pearson	Invalid	Inscribed as invalid under the 3d section of the act of May 1, 1820.
Benjamin Popkin		

PENSIONERS IN MASSACHUSETTS—Continued.

Names.	Acts under which restored.	Remarks.
William Parker, 4th	March 1, 1823	
James Paul	do	
Zenas Phinney	June 7, 1832	
John Paty		
John Pickens		
Sylvanus Pratt	do	
Ebenezer Peabody		
Benjamin Parker	do	
Elihu Pond	do	
James Pierce		
Benjamin Price	March 1, 1823	
John Pollard		
Samuel Pelton	June 7, 1832	
Lemuel Presson		
Thomas Peak		
Benjamin Paul	do	
Benjamin Pratt	March 1, 1823	
John Pierce	do	
Luther Pomeroy		
William Perkins	do	
Luke Packard	June 7, 1832	
Leonard Parks	do	
Paul Pratt		
Jedediah Phillips	do	
James Peck, 2d	March 1, 1823	
Nathaniel Pettee		
David Parker	June 7, 1823	
Abijah Pratt	do	
Timothy Perkins		
Philip Packard	March 1, 1823	
John Powers		
Joseph Paine	do	
Isaac Perkins	June 7, 1832	
Joseph Porter	do	
Lot Price		
Levi Proctor	March 1, 1823	
Joseph Powers		
Edward Phelps		
Philips Peirce		
Oliver Plimpton		
Imla Parker		
William Pincin	do	
William Park		
Timothy Palmer		
Gaius Pomeroy		
Amariah Preston	do	
James Russell		
Zacheus Rich	May 20, 1830	
Job Richardson		
Seth Ross	June 7, 1832	
Thomas Robbins	March 1, 1823	
William Ropes	do	
John Rogers, 1st	do	Relinquished for an increase of his stipend under the act of the 15th May, 1828.
Benjamin Richardson	June 7, 1832	
Daniel Robinson	March 1, 1823	
Abner Russell		
Lemuel Ross		
Samuel Reed, 2d		
Aaron Rogers	June 7, 1832	
Seth Rawson		
Lemuel Robinson		

[Doc. No. 127.] 43

PENSIONERS IN MASSACHUSETTS—Continued.

Names.	Acts under which restored.	Remarks.
Abijah Richardson, 2d	March 1, 1823	
Silas Roper		
Abijah Reed	do	
Giles Rider	do	
Levi Robinson	May 15, 1828	
Jacob Read		
Luke Robbins	March 1, 1823	
Job Ransom		
Enos Runnels	June 7, 1832	
William Roberts		
Peter Rogers		
Smith Rogers		
Jonathan Ring	March 3, 1819	Special act.
William Ripley	March 1, 1823	
Thomas Ross	June 7, 1832	
Daniel Ross	do	
Uriah Reed	do	
Anthony Remington	March 1, 1823	
Moses Rawson		
Levi Rose		
Samuel Rowe	do	
James Ross	do	
Josiah Richardson		
Zephaniah Robinson	do	
Ebenezer Reed	June 7, 1832	
Benjamin Rowley		
Samuel Root	May 15, 1828	
Abijah Richardson		
Abel Richardson	March 1, 1823	
John Runey		
Samuel Robins	June 7, 1832	
Joseph Robinson		
Zephaniah Ross	May 20, 1830	
Isaac Stone	March 1, 1823	
William Sizer		
Jeduthan Stevens	June 7, 1832	
William Simpson		
James Snow	do	
Ebed Stodder	do	
Josiah Stickney		
John Spaulding	do	
Benjamin Stewart		
Edward Smith	do	
Caleb Segers	March 1, 1823	
Joseph Sever	do	
David L. Shields	May 15, 1828	
Daniel Stevenson		
Habakkuk Stearns		
Benjamin Sanders	June 7, 1832	
James Smiley		
Nathan Snow	do	
John Sweet		
Isaac Smith		
Benjamin Sherman	do	
Obed Shaw	do	
Consider Studley	March 1, 1823	
Samuel Stodard	May 15, 1828	
Ebenezer Snow		
Solomon Snow	June 7, 1832	
Eli Simons		
Darius Stebbins		
Moses Stanfo.d		

[Doc. No. 127.]

PENSIONERS IN MASSACHUSETTS—Continued.

Names.	Acts under which restored.	Remarks.
Samuel Sherman		
Nehemiah Smith		
John Spear		
John Smith, 2d	May 15, 1828	
John Smith, 1st		
Jeremiah Smith	March 1, 1823	
Nathan Story		
Amos Sargent	do.	
Daniel Silver	June 7, 1832	
Joseph Shadduck	do.	
Studley Sampson	do.	
Liffee Smith	do.	
Robert Steele	May 15, 1828	
Joseph Souther		
Ebenezer Snow, 2d		
Joel Silvester	March 1, 1823	
Nathaniel Snow	do.	
Nathan Shippe		
Eli Smith	June 7, 1832	
John Sherman	March 1, 1823	
Nahum Smith		
Joseph Sanford	June 7, 1832	
Crocker Sampson		
Heman Sturtevant		
Abner Sampson	do.	
Rufus Sherman	do.	
David Shurtleff	do.	
Nathan Sears		
Caleb Stetson		
Colson Sampson	do.	
Benjamin Southwick	March 1, 1823	
Henry Story	- -	In this case the pensioner never exhibited a schedule of his property; but his pension was stopped because the Department was informed that he was not in needy circumstances.
Nathaniel Spooner		
Roswell Strong	June 7, 1832	
Samuel Sprague		
William Starr		
Peter Sears		
Edward Smothers		
Ahira Samson		
Lemuel Smith	do.	
Amos Sampson	do.	
John Smith		
Solomon Sargeant	March 1, 1823	
Samuel Sampson	June 7, 1832	
James Stodder	do.	
Moses Sprague		
Samuel Shaw		
Oliver Smith	March 1, 1823	
Amos Sheldon		
William Sheldon		
Simeon Spear		
Silas Stetson		
Gideon Stetson	June 7, 1832	
Samuel Sargent		
Amos Standish	do.	
Ebenezer Standish	do.	
Robert Sprout	do.	
Daniel Salley	do.	

[Doc. No. 127] 45

PENSIONERS IN MASSACHUSETTS—Continued.

Names.	Acts under which restored.	Remarks.
Nathaniel Standish		
John Smith		
Charles Stearns		
Jesse Smith, 2d		
Reuben Sheldon	June 7, 1832	
Isaac Sanderson	do.	
Jacob Smith	March 1, 1823	
Nathaniel Torrey		
Ephraim Temple	June 7, 1832	
Thomas Twitchell		
Thomas Thorp	March 1, 1823	
Jeffry Thissell		
Thomas Thompson		
Eliakim Tufts		
Oliver Train		
Amos Thayer, 1st		
Solomon Thayer	June 7, 1832	
William Thorning		
Lewis Taylor	May 15, 1828	
William Taylor	do.	
Willard Thomas	March 1, 1823	
Salmon Temple	do.	
Josiah Taft	do.	
Thomas Tupper		
Plato Turner		
William Tryon		
David Tufts		
Nathaniel Trask	do	Relinquished for an increase of his stipend, under the act of June 7, 1832.
Zacheus Thayer		
Samuel Taylor, 2d		
Solomon Twist	do.	Relinquished for an increase of his stipend under the act of June 7, 1832.
Ichabod Tupper		
David Tarr, 2d		
Daniel Talbot		
James Tisdale	do.	Relinquished for an increase of his stipend, under the act of May 15, 1828.
Stephen Totman	do.	
Elisha Turner		
Leander Toulong		
Isaac Thomas		
John Townsend	June 7, 1832	
Benjamin Todd	March 1, 1823	
Amos Thayer, 2d	do.	
Jacob Tyrill	June 7, 1832	
Enos Taft	do.	
Ichabod Tilson		
Randall Thayer		
Cornelius Tilleston	do.	
William Taylor		
Tertius Taylor		
Dan Townley	do.	
John Tucker	March 1, 1823	
Samuel Twiss	June 7, 1832	
Moses Thompson	do.	
Joshua Thomas		
Jonathan Taylor, 2d	do.	
Josiah Thomson, 1st		
Elias D. Trafton		
Samuel Taylor	do.	
John Trumbull	do.	

[Doc. No. 127.]

PENSIONERS IN MASSACHUSETTS—Continued.

Names.	Acts under which restored.	Remarks.
Nelson Thomas		
Benoni Twitchell		
Ebenezer Taft	June 7, 1832	
William Torrey	May 15, 1828	
Mathew Tower	March 1, 1823	
Jonathan Turner		
Nathaniel Tremain	June 7, 1832	
William Tilton		
Asa Thayer	March 1, 1823	
Thomas Thissell	do.	
John Union		
Nathan Underwood	do.	
Samuel Utley		
George Vining		
Joshua Vincent	June 7, 1832	
John Vose		
Henry Wright	March 1, 1823	
Christopher Ward		
Ephraim Warren		
Jacob Wales		
Caleb Wood	June 7, 1832	
Ely Wood		
Zacheus Watkins		
Ebenezer Whitney, 1st	March 1, 1823	
Israel Woodbury	June, 7, 1832	
Robert Woodbury	March 1, 1823	
Jonathan Woodman	do.	
John Woods	May 15, 1828	
Asa Winter		
Benjamin Witt		
Joseph Wiggins		
Robert Walker	do.	
Isaac Wright	March 1, 1823	
Timothy Wilder	do.	
George Webb	do.	
John Woolridge	do.	
Stephen Watkins	June 7, 1832	
Samuel Wheeler	do.	
Abijah Wood	do.	
Joshua Wardwell		
Samuel Warfield	do.	
Jason Walker	March 1, 1823	
Jonathan Warren		
Hezekiah Wheeler	May 15, 1828	
Alexander Wheelock		
Jacob B. Woodbury	June 7, 1832	
Elias Wair		
Samuel Weeks	do.	
Thomas Wood		
Ezekiel Wilcox		
Eleazer Webster		
Russell Wheeler		
Levi White	March 1, 1823	
William Winchester	June 7, 1832	
Enoch Whitmore	May 15, 1828	
Peter Willard		
Thomas Webb		
Smith White		
Paul Warner	March 1, 1823	
Joshua Warfield	do.	
Caleb Whiting		
Joseph Willis	do.	

PENSIONERS IN MASSACHUSETTS Continued.

Names.	Acts under which restored.	Remarks.
Jacob Weld		
James Woodman	June 7, 1832	
Martin Weller		
Stephen Wyatt		
Thomas Welch	March 1, 1823	
Ebenezer Willis		
David Wells	June 7, 1832	
Shubal Wilder	do.	
Thomas Weatherbee	March 1, 1823	
Ebenezer Withington	June 7, 1832	
Elias Warner	do.	
Peter Weber		
Benjamin Walcut		
Asa Waters	do.	
Ebenezer Wyeth	March 1, 1823	
David Whitman	do.	
James Wheeler	June 7, 1832	
Asa Williams	March 1, 1823	
Samuel Wood	do.	
Robert Williams	May 15, 1828	
Nichols Wood	March 1, 1823	
Lettice Washburn	do.	
Micah White	June 7, 1832	
Daniel White		
Timothy Whiting		
Obadiah Wickett		
Samuel White, 2d	March 1, 1823	
Reuben Wharfield	June 7, 1832	
James Walker		
Simon Whitney		
William Ward	do.	
Nicholas Ward	do.	
Luke White	do.	
Joshua Walbridge	do.	
Abel Wilder	- -	In this case the pensioner never exhibited a schedule of his property; but his pension was stopped because the department was informed that he was not in needy circumstances.
Jonathan Woodcock		
Nahum Wight	Invalid	Restored to invalid roll, under the 3d section of the act of May 1, 1820; also on roll under the act of June 7, 1832.
Henry Wotton		
Abisha Weeks		
Charles Willis		
David Whipple, 2d	March 1, 1823	
Joseph Whiting	June 7, 1832	
Nathan Wait		
Ebenezer Wright	March 1, 1823	
Nathan Weaver	do.	
Richard Walker	June 7, 1832	
Ely Wing		
Nathaniel Wade		
Isaac Whitmore	March 1, 1823	
Daniel Woodward	June 7, 1832	
Abel Winship	March 1, 1823	
Topsail Woodward		
Elias Ware	Invalid	Restored to invalid roll, under the 3d section of the act of May 1, 1820; again pensioned under the act of March 1, 1823.
Benjamin Woodbury	March 1, 1823	

PENSIONERS IN MASSACHUSETTS—Continued.

Names.	Acts under which restored.	Remarks.
Joshua Wright	March 1, 1823	
Benjamin Webber	do.	
Isaac Williams, 2d	do.	
James Walker	June 7, 1832	
Israel Wing	March 1, 1823	
Samuel Whitney	do.	
Silas Whitaker	do.	
Joseph Young		
Henry Young		
John Young		

[Doc. No. 127.]   49

PENSIONERS in Rhode Island who have been dropped from the pension roll under the act of 1st May, 1820; prepared in conformity with the resolution of the House of Representatives of the United States of the 17th December, 1835.

Names.	Acts under which restored.	Remarks.
Joseph Arnold	June 7, 1832	
Thomas Angles		
Benjamin Boss	do.	
Christopher Chester	March 1, 1823	
James Chappell	Invalid	Restored under 3d section of the act of 1st of May, 1820.
James Crandal	March 1, 1823	
John Crandell		
Amherst Crandall	do.	
John Elliott	Invalid	Restored under 3d section of the act of 1st of May, 1820.
Nathaniel Elliott	May 20, 1830	
Richard Guild	March 1, 1823	
John George		
Benjamin Knight	do.	
Samuel Lewis		
David Maxfield	do.	
Jeremiah Niles	do.	
Henry Northup		
Benjamin Peck	do.	
William Page		
Job Page	do.	
Peter Penno		
Nathaniel Phillips		
Daniel Pierce	do.	
Robert Rogers	do.	Relinquished for an increase of his stipend, under act of the 7th June, 1832.
William Read	do.	
James Reynolds	June 7, 1832	
Ichabod Simmons	March 1, 1823	
John Spurr	do.	
Peter Turner		
Henry Tabor		
James Wallace		
William Waterman		
John Yeomans		
Elias Young	June 7, 1832	

4

[Doc. No. 127.]

PENSIONERS in Connecticut who have been dropped from the pension roll under the act of May 1, 1820, prepared in conformity with the resolution of the House of Representatives, of the 17th December, 1835.

Names.	Acts under which restored.	Remarks.
Luke Adams	March 1, 1823	
Stephen Alling	do.	
Abel Abell	June 7, 1832	
Abel Alling	March 1, 1823	
Othniel Allen		
Aaron Abbott	do.	
Thomas Ackley	May 15, 1828	
William Ashcraft	March 1, 1823	
John Andrus		
Josiah Andrus	do.	
Daniel Allen	do.	
Daniel Averil	June 7, 1832	
Arnold Allen	do.	
James Anderson, 2d	March 1, 1823	
David Allen	May 15, 1828	
Joseph Ashley	June 7, 1832	
Samuel Aborn		
John Allen	May 15, 1828	
Walter Booth	March 1, 1823	
Daniel Bradley		
Christopher Bailey	June 7, 1832	
Ephraim Bailey		
Ephraim Bowers	March 1, 1823	
Benanuel Bonfoy		
Amos Barnum	do.	
William Bacon	May 15, 1828	
London Bailey		
Zealous Blakeley		
Nathan Burnham, 1st	March 1, 1823	
Benjamin Butler		
Joseph Bunnell		
Hezekiah Brewster		
Daniel Buckley		
Orange Barnes		
Henry Brown		
Andrew Bostwick	March 1, 1823	
Geordon Bingham		
John Blackmore		
Sylvanus Badlam	May 15, 1828	
James Bartholomew	March 1, 1823	Relinquished for an increase of his stipend under the act of June 7, 1832.
William Bennett	do.	
Benjamin Brockway	- - -	Restored to invalid roll under 3d section of the act of 1st May, 1820. Again restored under act 1st March, 1823.
John Bishop		
Stephen Betts	May 15, 1828	
Grove Barnard		
Samuel Blackman	March 1, 1823	
Daniel Bradley	do.	Relinquished for an increase of his stipend under act 15th May, 1828.
Stephen Batterson	do.	
Jacob Bishop	June 7, 1832	
Hezekiah Betts	March 1, 1823	Relinquished for an increase of his stipend under act 7th June, 1832.
Ezekiel P. Belden		
John Bissel		
Thomas F. Bishop	June 7, 1832	

[Doc. No. 127.]

PENSIONERS IN CONNECTICUT—Continued.

Names.	Acts under which restored.	Remarks.
Zachariah Blakeman	June 7, 1832	
Joseph Beckwith	March 1, 1823	
Beriah Babcock	do.	Relinquished for an increase of his stipend under the act of June 7, 1832.
Thaddeus Beach	do.	
Deodate Beaumont	do.	
Isaac Beers	do.	
Elkanah Barton	do.	
Charles Buckley	June 7, 1832	
Nathaniel Brooks		
Samuel Bliss	do.	
Gilead Bradley	do.	
Barah Benson	do.	
Rozzel Bill	March 1, 1823	
Israel Barnes	June 7, 1832	
James Bevis	do.	
John Blackleach		
Jesse Breed		
Henry Burbeck	May 15, 1828	
Esaias Butts	March 1, 1823	
Aaron Benjamin	do.	Relinquished for an increase of his stipend under act 15th May, 1828.
Edward Bassett	—	Restored to invalid roll under 3d section act 1st May, 1828.
Benjamin Chittenden		
Abner Chapman	June 7, 1832	
Josiah Chatfield	March 1, 1823	
George Clark	do.	
John Chittenden		
Samuel Camp		
Samuel Chamberlain		
Giles Clark	do.	
Jedediah Chapman	do.	Relinquished for an increase of his stipend under the act of the 7th of June, 1832.
Abner Cole		
William Clark		
Levi Chatfield		
Robert Clark		
Josiah Cleveland		
Ezra Clark	do.	
Thomas Church	June 7, 1832	
Samuel Cluxton		
Asa Copland	May 15, 1828	
Elijah Chapman	March 1, 1823	
Nathaniel Crittenden	do.	
Earl Clapp	do.	Relinquished for an increase of his stipend under the act of the 7th of June, 1832.
Squire Cady	June 7, 1832	
Ebenezer Copp	March 1, 1823	
Jacob Cleaveland		
Sylvanus Conant	June 7, 1832	
Israel Cone		
James Chapman	do.	
Asa Cowles	March 1, 1823	
Silas Chaplain	June 7, 1832	
Eli Curtis		
Abner Cable	do.	
Theodore alias Theodorus Chamberlain		
Lemuel Caswell	March 1, 1823	
Ebenezer Chapman		
Comfort Carpenter		

[Doc. No. 127.]

PENSIONERS IN CONNECTICUT—Continued.

Names.	Acts under which restored.	Remarks.
Eliphalet Corbin	March 1, 1823	
Collins Chapman	do.	
Elisha Clark	- -	Restored to invalid roll under 3d section of the act of May 1, 1820. Also on roll under act 7th June, 1832, in conformity with the act of February 19, 1833.
Reuben Champion	do.	
Samuel Comstock		
Levi Clark		
Flavel Clark	June 7, 1832	
Uriah Church		
Thomas Chaffee		
Obadiah Church		
Nathan Coleman		
Oliver Comstock		
David Canada		
Augustus Curtis	do.	
Joel Chaffee	do.	
Thomas Coe		
Richard Dond		
Stephen De Wolf	March 1, 1823	
Jedediah Dennison	June 7, 1832	
Bishop Dodd		
Joel Doane	March 1, 1823	
Israel Driggs		
Levi De Wolf	June 7, 1832	
Amasa Dimmick	March 1, 1823	
Samuel Dean	do.	
Stephen Dunham	June 7, 1832	
Stephen B. Davis	March 1, 1823	
Edward Dunscombe	do.	
Phineas Dean	June 7, 1832	
Ebor Dudley	do.	
Daniel Darrow		
Henry Daggett, jr.	May 15, 1828	
Phineas Drake	June 7, 1832	
Oliver Dutton		
John Eldridge		
Gilbert Edgecomb	do.	
Daniel Everest		
Benjamin Elsworth		
Chancy Foster		
Edward Fields		
Jonathan Finch		
Samuel Frothingham	do.	
James Fuller		
Timothy Freeman	do.	
Eli Fuller		
Philemon Freeman		
John Fanning		
Jonathan Fuller		
Solomon Fenton	do.	
Abijah Fuller	March 1, 1823	
Peter Fairfield		
Abel French	June 7, 1832	
Midian Griswold		
Gideon Goff	May 15, 1828	
Bildad Granger		
Ichabod Goodrich	March 1, 1823	
Joseph Gould		
George Griswold	do.	Relinquished for an increase of his stipend under the act of June 7, 1832.

[Doc. No. 127.] 53
PENSIONERS IN CONNECTICUT—Continued.

Names.	Acts under which restored.	Remarks.
Zenas Griswold	June 7, 1832	
Daniel Galpin	March 1, 1823	Relinquished for an increase of his stipend under act of June 7, 1832.
Thomas Grosvenor		
Joseph Giddings	March 1, 1823	
Moore Gibbs	May 15, 1828	
Joel Gillett		
George Gear		
Simon Giffin		
Benjamin Greenslet		
Silas Goodell		
Selah Griswold	June 7, 1832	
John Griffin	March 1, 1823	
Joseph Gladding		
Benjamin Gilbert	June 7, 1832	
Moses Goodman		
Amos Galpin	do.	
Josiah Gary		
John Gellet	May 15, 1828	
James Goodrich	June 7, 1832	
Asa Griswold		
Benjamin Gidding		
Asa Gilbert	do.	
Ephraim Gillett	March 1, 1823	
Othniel Gillet	do.	
Aaron Hall	June 7, 1832	
Benajah Hall	March 1, 1823	
Jairus Harrison		
Joseph Hoyt		
Hezekiah Hawley		
Zaphariah Hull	do.	Relinquished for an increase of his stipend under act June 7, 1832.
Cornelius Higgins	June 7, 1832	
Ebenezer Hinckley	March 1, 1823	Relinquished for an increase of his stipend under act June 7, 1832.
Crippon Hurd, jr.	do.	
Eliada Hitchcock	do.	
Roger Hooker		
Thomas Huntley		
Thomas Hallet	May 15, 1828	
Alexander Hyde	March 1, 1823	
Elisha Horton	May 15, 1828	
John Hilliard		
Zenas Haws	March 1, 1823	
Cornelius Hamlin	do.	
Samuel Hait	May 15, 1828	
Elnathan Hurd	June 7, 1832	
Salmon Hubbell	May 15, 1828	
Benjamin Howard	June 7, 1832	
Ebenezer Hoadley	May 15, 1828	
Eliphalet Holmes	March 1, 1823	Relinquished for an increase of his stipend under act June 7, 1832.
Titus Harlor Heart	June 7, 1832	
Ebenezer Huntington	March 1, 1823	Relinquished for an increase of his stipend under act 15th May, 1828.
Joseph Hatch	March 1, 1823	
Medad Hotchkiss		
Daniel Hitchcock	May 15, 1828	
Hezekiah Herenden	March 1, 1823	
Hezekiah Hine		
Levi Hotchkiss		
Theodore Harrison	June 7, 1832	

PENSIONERS IN CONNECTICUT—Continued.

Names.	Acts under which restored.	Remarks.
Isaac Hotchkiss	June 7, 1832	
Joel House	do.	
William Hooker		
Benjamin Hart		
Ebenezer Hanford	do.	
John Harron		
Thaddeus Husled	do.	
Abner Hill		
Ebenezer Hoyt	March 1, 1823	
David Harris	do.	
Bliss Hart		
Elias Hart	June 7, 1832	
Ager Hyde		
Levi Hitchcock		
Jonathan Holt	March 1, 1823	
James Hawley	do.	
Jonathan Hazleton	do.	
Stephen Judd		
Deodate Pratt Jones	do.	
Joseph Jones	June 7, 1832	
Briggs Ingersoll		
George Justin	March 1, 1823	
Daniel Jackway	do.	
Morris Jones		
James Johnson	June 7, 1832	
Eaton Jones	do.	
John Isham	do.	
Burrett Jennings	March 1, 1823	
Alpheus Kingsley	do.	
Abraham T. Kimball	do.	
Jonathan Knight	do.	Relinquished for an increase of his stipend under the act of the 15th of May, 1828.
Joseph Kingsbury		
William Lord		
Samuel Lord	March 1, 1823	
Ebenezer Lester	do.	
Samuel Loomis	–	Restored to Invalid roll under the 3d section of the act of the 1st of May, 1820.
Isaac Lookwood	June 7, 1832	
Jonathan Luce	May 15, 1828	
David Lawrence	March 1, 1823	
Dean Lee	do.	
James Lamphier		
Jedediah Leach	March 1, 1823	
Rufus Landon	June 7, 1832	
Richard Law	do.	
William Lockwood	May 15, 1828	
Ezra Lee		
John Lawrence	do.	
Simeon Lincoln		
Solomon Loring	June 7, 1832	
Silas Lamb	March 1, 1823	
John Mansfield		
Elisha Munson	June 7, 1832	
Caleb Miller	May 15, 1828	
Ebenezer Mansfield		
Joseph Mason	March 1, 1823	
John Meigs		
Amasa Mills		
Elisha Mason	June 7, 1832	
Reuben Messenger	March 1, 1823	
Joseph Minor	June 7, 1832	

[Doc. No. 127.] 55

PENSIONERS IN CONNECTICUT—Continued.

Names.	Acts under which restored.	Remarks.
Stephen Munson		
Uriah Mead	May 15, 1828	
Joseph Mansfield		
Nathaniel Markham		
Goddard Martinus		
Levitt Millard	June 7, 1832	
John Miles	May 15, 1828	
Ebenezer Morgan	March 1, 1823	
Nathaniel Martin	June 7, 1832	
David Mallery	March 1, 1823	
Samuel B. Marshall		
Joseph Martin	do.	
Aaron Mills		
Elisha Niles		
Joshua Newhall		
Elisha Noble	do.	
Mark Newell		
David Nevens		
Seth North		
Henry Norris	do.	
Levi Norton		
Abraham Nott or Knott	do.	
Stephen Osborne		
Jeremiah Osborn		
Daniel Putnam		
John Peck	May 15, 1828	
Joseph Porter		
Benjamin Potter	do.	
Joel Potter	March 1, 1823	
Joseph Peck	June 7, 1832	
Isaac Palmer		
Edward Pellom		
Richard Price		
Jesse Peck		
Dan Platts		
John Pierpont	May 15, 1828	
John Parker	March 1, 1823	
Thomas Powers		
William Phillips	do.	
Thomas Pool		
Frederick Pearl	do.	
Abraham Perkins	do.	
Samuel Phelps		
Ward Peck	May 15, 1828	
William Plumbe	do.	
Absalom Pride	June 7, 1832	
Ammi Paulk	March 1, 1823	Relinquished for an increase of his stipend under the act of the 7th of June, 1832.
Lysias Peck	do.	
John Packer, 2d	do.	
Nathaniel Perry	do.	
Ezra Porter		
Medad Potter	May 15, 1828	
Simeon Pease	June 7, 1832	
Ezra Potter	March 1, 1823	
David Phelps	June 7, 1832	
Pierce Packhurst	do.	
Elijah Porter	do.	
Ebenezer Platt		
Samuel Perry		
Samuel Perry, 2d		
Elias Pond	March 1, 1823	

PENSIONERS IN CONNECTICUT—Continued.

Names.	Acts under which restored.	Remarks.
Jasper Pratt		
Sherman Rowland	May 15, 1828	
Elijah Ransom		
Luther Reeves		
Elias Robinson	June 7, 1832	
Heman Rogers	March 1, 1823	
John Roberts		
Samuel Richards	May 15, 1828	
Josiah Rogers		
Stephen Rainey	do.	
Nathan Root	March 1, 1823	
Thomas Rogers	do.	
John Rowe	June 7, 1832	
Ezra Rowe	do.	
Benjamin Reed	do.	
Owen Ruick		
Leonard Rogers	March 1, 1823	Relinquished for an increase of his stipend under the act of the 7th of June, 1832.
Moses Riggs	do.	
John Russell	May 15, 1828	
Bostwick Ruggles		
Ebenezer Robbins	June 7, 1832	
David Reynolds	do.	
Daniel Reedd		
Jesse Rowland		
Daniel Root	March 1, 1823	
Eber Stocking	May 15, 1828	
Abijah Savage		
Josiah Smith, 2d		
Jacob Strong	March 1, 1823	
Timothy Scranton		
John Smith, 1st		
Daniel Sizer	do.	
Joseph Sparkes		
David Spencer	do.	Relinquished for an increase of his stipend under the act of June 7, 1832.
Elias Stevens	June 7, 1832	
Elias Stillwell		
Aaron Simons		
Lycus Simons		
Samuel Scovel	do.	
Abisha Smith	do.	
Daniel Stoddard	do.	
Thomas Stone	May 15, 1828	
Reuben Sharp	June 7, 1832	
Nehemiah Storer		
Joseph Snell	March 1, 1823	
John Smith, 3d	May 15, 1828	
George Seymour		
Strong Sanford	do.	
Roger Stillman	June 7, 1832	
William Shattock	do.	
Jonathan Sizer	do.	
Abner Slade	do.	
Samuel Stowell	March 1, 1823	
Ephraim Spencer		
Henry Stevens	do.	
Adonijah St. John	do.	
Moses Sturges		
Joseph Seeley	do.	
Jesse St. John	May 15, 1828	
Seth Savage	June 7, 1832	

PENSIONERS IN CONNECTICUT—Continued.

Names.	Acts under which restored	Remarks.
Asaph Smith		
Enoch Smith	June 7, 1832	
Elijah Seldon		
Jeremiah Smith	do.	
Benjamin Stevens	March 1, 1823	Relinquished for an increase of his stipend, under the act of the 7th of June, 1832.
Thaddeus Starr	June 7, 1832	
Jesse Shepperd		
William Smith	do.	
Gideon Sikes	do.	
Theodore Spencer	March 1, 1823	Relinquished for an increase of his stipend, under act of June 7, 1832.
Elihu Sanford	May 15, 1828	
Joseph Seagrave		
Ralph Smith		
Nathaniel Swift		
Jacob Scovil	March 1, 1823	
Anthony Strong		
John Tyler		
John Treat		
Lemuel Tuttle	March 1, 1823	
Earl Tharp	do.	
Abner Tibbetts	do.	
James Tooker		
William Tryon		
David Taylor, 2d		
Abraham Thompson		
Dudley Tracy	do.	
Amos Tharp		
Ezekiel Trumbull	do.	
Benjamin Treadwell	do.	
Gamaliel R. Tracy	June 7, 1832	
William Taylor	May 15, 1828	
Thomas Tibbles		
Daniel Thomas	June 7, 1832	
Samuel Thompson	March 1, 1823	
John Thompson		
Chester Upham		
John Villard		
Jehiel Wilcox	March 1, 1823	
Simeon Wells	do.	Relinquished for an increase of his stipend, under act of June 7, 1832.
William Weare		
Jacob Wardwell		
Moses Webb	do.	
John Waterbury		
Elijah Wilcox	do.	
Simeon Webster	do.	
John Wright	do.	
Benjamin Wright		
Philip White	May 15, 1828	
Ephraim White	June 7, 1832	
William Wamsly		
Robert Westland		
Samuel Waugh	May 15, 1828	
Hopestill Welch	March 1, 1823	
Thomas Wainwright		
Abraham Waid		
John R. Watrous	May 15, 1828	
Charles Walter	March 1, 1823	
Abraham Wheadon	June 7, 1832	
Nathaniel Walker		

PENSIONERS IN CONNECTICUT—Continued.

Names.	Acts under which restored.	Remarks.
Reynolds Webb	June 7, 1832	
Rufus Wheedon		
Joseph Whiting		
James Wickwire		
John Webb		
John Wilson	do.	
Samuel Whiting	March 1, 1823	
Nathan Wilcox	do.	
Charles Wright		
Thomas Weaver		
John Welch	do.	
Abner Wooden	June 7, 1832	
John Weed	do.	
Thomas Wilder	do.	
John Warren, 2d		
Nathan Williams	do.	
John Warner, 2d		Restored to invalid roll, under the 3d section of the act of May 1, 1820.
Isaac Way	March 1, 1823	
Moses Young	June 7, 1832	

PENSIONERS in New York who have been dropped from the pension roll under the act of 1st May, 1820, prepared in conformity with the resolution of the House of Representatives of the 17th December, 1835.

Names.	Acts under which restored.	Remarks.
David Atkins	May 15, 1828	
David Adams	March 1, 1823	
John Ames	do.	
Emanuel Adams	do.	
Thomas Adams	June 7, 1832	
Nathan Allen		
John Austin		
William Andruss, jr.	March 1, 1823	
Thomas Armsbury		
Eusebius Austin	do.	
Daniel Avery		
Phinehas Austin		
Abraham Avery	June 7, 1832	
Daniel Ashley		
Joseph Anderson	do.	
Daniel Alvord	March 1, 1823	
Edward Annable	do.	
Richard Anderson	May 15, 1828	
Daniel Angel	June 7, 1832	
William Bardsley	May 15, 1828	
Joseph Bond		
Elias Bixby	March 1, 1823	
John Butler	June 7, 1832	
Walter Bicker		
Oliver Bowers	March 1, 1823	
Matthew Bennet	do.	
John Bostwick	June 7, 1832	
Ithamar Bouker		
Jacob Bamper		
Charles Burritt	March 1, 1823	
John Burgis		
William Baker, 1st		
Isaac Buell	Invalid	Restored to invalid roll under the 3d section of the act of the 1st of May, 1820.
Elisha Burdick	May, 15, 1828	
Henry Burdick	March 1, 1823	
William Bacon		
Zephaniah Branch	–	In this case the pension was stopped because the department was informed that the pensioner was not in needy circumstances.
John Bodwell	do.	
Samuel Brown, 5th	do.	
Elijah Bryan	May 5, 1823	
Jacob Boyers	March 1, 1823	
Samuel Bates		
William Blake		
Edward Butterick		
Isaiah Betts	do.	
Dan Blackman	do.	
Thompson Burdick	do.	
Gideon Ball	do.	
Samuel Bissell		
Gilbert Brush		
John Bowles		
Ebenezer Ballentine		
John Bentley		
Daniel Bissell		

[Doc. No. 127.]

PENSIONERS IN NEW YORK—Continued.

Names.	Acts under which restored.	Remarks.
Solomon Blodget	June 7, 1832	
Jonathan Barnes	March 1, 1823	
Sylvanus Bishop	June 7, 1832	
Joseph Brown, 2d	do.	
Jacob Bennett		
Isaac Bartholomew	May 15, 1828	
John Barber	June 7, 1832	
Isaac Bennett		
Austin Brown	May 15, 1828	
John Bell	June 7, 1832	
Ebenezer Bacon	do.	
Alexander Beebe	do.	
Silas Bling		
John Bowen	do.	
Jarib Bacon	March 1, 1823	
Timothy S. Barton	June 7, 1832	
Jonathan Barton	March 1, 1823	
Nathaniel Bird		
Lewis Baker	June 7, 1832	
John Baxter, 2d	do.	
Silas Brooks	May 15, 1828	
Abraham Boileau		
Hozea Birge	- -	In this case the pensioner never exhibited a schedule of his property; but his pension was stopped because the department was informed that he was not in needy circumstances. Afterwards inscribed on roll under the act of 7th June, 1832.
Henry Bonfy	June 7, 1832	
James Brown	March 1, 1823	
Israel Beach	June 7, 1832	
Samuel Brown, 4th		
John Beall		
Jonathan Ball		
Samuel Blackman	March 1, 1823	
Abel Belknap	June 7, 1832	
Orrin Burnham	do.	
Eleazer Baker	do.	
Ebenezer Burnet		
Andrew Bell	do.	
Moses Blakely	do.	
Aaron Bullard	March 1, 1823	
Michael Burge	do,	Relinquished for an increase of his stipend under the act of 7th June, 1832.
Phineas Bell	do.	
Cornelius Baldwin	June 7, 1832	
John Blanchard		
John Bump	March 1, 1823	
Abner Buck	do.	
Daniel Barnum	do.	
Thomas Chipman	do.	
Cyrus Cartwright	do.	
Shubal Cunningham	do.	
Benjamin Clough	do.	
Elijah Chapman		
Eliphalet Chiney		
Edward Currin		
Jabez Colt		
Matthew Clark		
Lemuel Cook	June 7, 1832	
Jonas Clark	March 1, 1823	
Thomas Corbet	do.	

PENSIONERS IN NEW YORK—Continued.

Names.	Acts under which restored.	Remarks.
Nicholas Cusick	May 15, 1828	
William Chevers		
Samuel Cole	June 7, 1832	
Seth Capron	do.	
Richard Cooke	do.	
David Cornell		
Nehemiah Cleaveland	do.	
Peter Covert	March 1, 1823	
Benjamin Camp	June 7, 1832	
Robert Castle	do.	
James Covel	do.	
Richard Carter	do.	In this case the pensioner never exhibited a schedule of his property, but his pension was stopped because the department was informed that he was not in needy circumstances.
Amariah Crane	March 1, 1823	
Samuel Cook		
Kenneth Campbell	May 15, 1828	
Amos Conant	March 1, 1823	
Stephen Clapp	May 15, 1828	
John Chambers	June 7, 1832	
Eliphalet Clark	March 1, 1823	
Willard Church		
Ebenezer Covill	June 7, 1832	
Amos Clark, 1st		
Joel Clark	May 15, 1828	
Joseph Collins	March 1, 1823	
Stephen Corbin	June 7, 1832	
William Cook, 2d		
James Croft	do.	
Benjamin Covel		
Benjamin Curtis		
John Cochran		
Jared Chittenden		
Benjamin Chamberlain	March 1, 1823	
Joseph Cross		
Peter Combe		
Benjamin Cornwell	do.	
David Cole	May 15, 1828	
John Cunningham		
Jonathan Crain		
Nathan Chandler	March 1, 1823	
George Champlin	do.	
Joseph Copp	May 15, 1828	
Thomas Cathcart	June 7, 1832	
William Cook, 3d	do.	
Roger Crain	do.	
Frederick Curtis		
Ezra Clawson	March 1, 1823	
Caleb Clark	June 7, 1832	
Daniel Couch	do.	
Aaron Chamberlain		
Oliver Collins	May 15, 1828	
Robert Carr		
Rowland Cotton	Invalid	Reinstated on invalid roll under the 3d section of the act of 1st May, 1820.
William Cleveland	June 7, 1832	
Edward Crumpston		
Joseph Crandall	do.	
Asa Cranson	do.	
Miles Cook	May 15, 1828	

PENSIONERS IN NEW YORK—Continued.

Names.	Acts under which restored.	Remarks.
Alexander Church	March 1, 1823	
Niles Coleman	do.	
Isaac Cooper		
Jonathan Crocker	do.	Special act.
Phinehas Dodge	June 7, 1832	
Josiah Doan	do.	
Lothario Donaldson	do.	
James Davis	do.	
Seth Doubleday	do.	
John Dunbar	do.	
Samuel Day	do.	
John Docker	March 1, 1823	
Samuel Doty	do.	
Oliver Drew	do.	
Jedediah Darbee	do.	
William Dodge	do.	
John Dodge, 1st	May 15, 1828	
George Denneger	March 1, 1823	
William Davis, 3d	do.	
Timothy Dunham	do.	
Reuben Dodge	do.	
Pardon Dolbee	do.	
Levi Dodge	May 15, 1828	
Isaac Doty	March 1, 1823	
Daniel Dorsey		
Thomas De Russy		
Benjamin Dimmick	May 15, 1828	
Perez Drake	March 1, 1823	
Benjamin Daball	do.	
Nathan Davis, 3d	do.	
David Dixon		
David Dorrance		
George Doolittle		
Jeremiah Dunham	May 15, 1828	
Thomas Dodge		
Samuel Downing		
John Dailey	March 1, 1823	
Joseph Davis	June 7, 1832	
Goldsmith Davis	March 1, 1823	
Chapman Davis	do.	
Joseph Delong	do.	
Prince Danford	May 15, 1828	
Daniel Denton		
Benjamin Doty		
George Dellaby		
Francis Dodge	March 1, 1823	
Nathan Estabrook	do.	
Daniel Everitt	do.	
Ezra Eaton	do.	
Stephen Earl	do.	
Benoni Evins		
Henry Entrot	May 15, 1828	
Silas Evans		
John Erwin, 2d	March 1, 1823	
Wells Ely	do.	
Shereuah Evans		
Nathan Evins		
David Frances	June 7, 1832	
Daniel Felton	do	
James Fuller	do.	
Conrad Frantz	May 15, 1828	
James Ferguson		

PENSIONERS IN NEW YORK—Continued.

Names.	Acts under which restored.	Remarks.
Jonathan Ford	March 1, 1823	
Samuel Fox	May 15, 1828	
Andrew Freeman	March 1, 1823	
William Fay		
James Fletcher		
Archelaus Fletcher	do.	
John Franks		
James Frazier	June 7, 1832	
Josiah Fuller	March 1, 1823	
Thomas Frink	do.	
Leonard Farwell		
Pardon Field		
Conrad Friday	May 15, 1828	
Jonathan Fisk	March 1, 1823	
James Field		
Jonathan Francis		
Joseph Fox		
Elijah Freeman	do.	
Joel Fox	Invalid roll	Restored as invalid under the 3d section of the act of 1st of May, 1820.
Samuel Giles	June 7, 1832	
Roswell Goodrich	do.	
Abel Goodrich	do.	
Francis Garvey	March 1, 1823	
Obadiah Gridley	do.	
Thomas Grill	May 15, 1828	
Ezekiel Goodale	March 1, 1823	
Luther Gates		
Jonathan Gaylord	do.	
Isaac G. Graham	May 15, 1828	
Isaac Guion		
Butler Gilbert		
Peter Gress	do.	
Thomas Gilligan		
Elijah Gardner		
Benjamin Gilbert		
Jabez Gibbs		
Jason Gay		
Gershom Gilbert		
James Gay	June 7, 1832	
Peter Graves		
John Griswold	March 1, 1823	
Simeon Griswold	June 7, 1832	
Sebee Granger	March 1, 1823	
Zachariah Green	Invalid act	Restored under 3d section act May 1, 1820.
Thomas Gardner	March 1, 1823	
John Gardner		
Kirkland Griffin		
Peter Gibbons		
Edward Goodyear	May 15, 1828	
James Gunnel		
Solomon Goodwin	March 1, 1823	Relinquished for an increase of his stipend under the act of June 7, 1832.
William Gould	do.	
Samuel Gordon	do.	
Asa Gage	do.	
Abraham Garrison		
Aquilla Giles		
Benjamin Hall, 2d	do.	Relinquished for an increase of his stipend under the act of June 7, 1832.
Peter Hunt	June 7, 1832	
William Hanks	do.	

PENSIONERS IN NEW YORK—Continued.

Names.	Acts under which restored.	Remarks.
Timothy Holsted	June 7, 1832	
Levi Hitchcock	do.	
Joseph Holsted	do.	
George Holt	do.	
Abijah Hubbell	do.	
Aaron Hart	do.	
Oliver Hatch	do.	
Jacob Hayden	March 1, 1823	
Isaac Hotchkiss	do.	
William Henson		
Samuel Hubbard	do.	
John Hartwell	do.	
Cornelius House	do.	
Elisha Hill	do.	
Oliver Hyde	do.	
Hendrick Higbee	do.	
John Hinckley	do.	
Silas Holbrook	do.	Relinquished for an increase of his stipend, under the act of June 7, 1832.
Noadiah Hubbard	do.	
Jonathan Hall	do.	
Ivory Holland		
Samuel Hyatt	do.	
Samuel Hicock		
George Hakes		
Moses Hall, 2d		
Reuben Hill	do.	
Thomas Hale		
John Holridge	do.	Relinquished for an increase of his stipend, under the act of May 15, 1828.
Timothy Humphrey		
Bezaleel Howe		
Humphrey Hunt	Invalid act	Restored under the 3d section of the act of May 1, 1820.
Benjamin Hall		
John Helmage		
Nathaniel Humphrey		
Uriah Hibbard		
Nathaniel Holmes	March 1, 1823	
Chester Hull	May 15, 1828	
David Haskell		
Zenus Hathway	do.	
Asa Hull		
Jonathan Hallett		
Ely Hull		
Jonathan Hurlbutt	March 1, 1823	
Lemuel Hitchcock		
Lemuel Herrick		
Han Jost Hess	Invalid	Restored under the 3d section of the act of May 1, 1820; also on the roll under the act of May 15, 1828, conformably to the provisions of the act of May 31, 1830.
Christopher Hutton	May 15, 1828	
Richard Hewitt		
George House		
William Harrington		
Israel Harriott	March 1, 1823	
John Howard		
Reuben Hale		
David Hunter		
Luther Halsey	May 15, 1828	
John Humphreys		

PENSIONERS IN NEW YORK—Continued.

Names.	Acts under which restored.	Remarks.
Asa Hamlin	March 1, 1823	
Amasa Holdridge		
Isaac Jones	June 7, 1832	
Nehemiah Jones	do.	
Jeremiah Jackson	do.	
John Ingalsbie	do.	
Nathaniel Johnson		
Patton Jackson		
Abraham Johnson, 2d	March 1, 1823	
Luther Johnson	June 7, 1832	
Thomas Jordon	March 1, 1823	
Thomas Jones	do.	
Samuel Johnston	do.	
John Jeffries		
Israel Johnson	May 15, 1828	
William Johnson, 4th	March 1, 1823	Relinquished for an increase of his stipend, under the act of June 7, 1232.
Samuel Jones, 4th	do.	
John Jaquish	May 15, 1828	
Joseph Jennings		
William Jacques	do.	
Samuel Jones, 5th	June 7, 1832	
Conrad Ittig	May 15, 1830	
John Jeremiah		
David Johnson, 3d	June 7, 1832	
Joseph B. Jennison	May 20, 1830	
William Knapp	June 7, 1832	
Martin Kellog	do.	
Martin Kertland	do.	
John Kennelly	March 1, 1823	
Phineas Kellog	do.	
Daniel Keyes		
Samuel Knapp	do.	
Joseph Ketchum		
William Keator	do.	
Thomas Kent		
Hannonus Knickerbocker		
Christian Koon		
Jeremiah Keeler		
Noah Kellogg		
Jason Kellogg		
Enoch Kellogg	do.	
Daniel Kinney	do.	
Isaac Keeler		
Joseph King, 1st		
John Keyes	- -	In this case the pensioner never exhibited a schedule of his property; but his pension was stopped because the department was informed that he was not in needy circumstances.
Joseph Latham	June 7, 1832	
Hooker Low	do.	
William Lake	do.	
John Luther	March 1, 1823	
Cromwell Luther	do.	
Israel Loomis		
James Lafranbois	do.	
Stephen Leonard	do.	
Jabez Lewis	May 15, 1828	
Henry Lozear	March 1, 1823	
Hozea Lyons		
John Legg	do.	
Justus Lewis	do.	

PENSIONERS IN NEW YORK—Continued.

Names.	Acts under which restored.	Remarks.
John Lawton	March 1, 1823	
Calvin Lazadell		
Daniel Lee		
Ebenezer Lewis		
Nathan Legg		
Benjamin Langdon	do.	
Helebiant Lozier	May 15, 1828	
William Lashbrook	do.	
Nathan Law	March 1, 1823	
John Luce		
William H. Lee		
James Little		
Henry Little	do.	
Thomas Lyon	Invalid	Restored to Invalid roll under the 3d section of the act of the 1st of May, 1820.
Lebbeus Loomis	May 15, 1828	
Daniel Lake	June 7, 1832	
Peter Lozier		
Samuel Lewis		
Consider Lucas		
John Lewis	March 1, 1823	
William Miller	June 7, 1832	
Enos Morse	do.	
Stephen Moulton	do.	
Salmon Moulton	do.	
Josiah Mosher	do.	
Christopher Monk	do.	
Isaac Markham	do.	
Christopher McManus		
Martin McNeary	March 1, 1823	
Amos Muzzy	do.	
William Miller, 2d	June 7, 1832	
Ichabod Murray	March 1, 1823	
Jabez Matthews		
Jacob Multor	do.	
Joseph Morrell	do.	Relinquished for an increase of his stipend, under the act of May 15, 1828.
John McHugh	do.	
Lewis Moffet	do.	
Charles McDonald		
Patrick McGee		
Isaac Morrell		
Elisha Mix	do.	
Thodore May		
Asa Morrill	do.	
Nash Mitchell		
Orange Munson	do.	
Simeon Meacham	do.	
Garrit Marselis	May 15, 1828	
Andrew Murray		
Joseph Morgan, 2d		
Jeremiah Meacham		
Samuel Mills	March 1, 1823	
George McCutchen	May 15, 1828	
David Morss	do.	
Adam McNnight	June 7, 1832	
Matthew Marvin		
Roger Merrill		
Joseph Morgan	May 15, 1828	
Ashbell Mason	March 1, 1823	
Bazaleel Moffitt		
Richard Nixon	June 7, 1832	

[Doc. No. 127.]

PENSIONERS IN NEW YORK—Continued.

Names.	Acts under which restored.	Remarks.
Zenas Northway	June 7, 1832	
Epaphras Nott	do.	
George Norton		
Jonathan Newman		
Nathan Nichols		
Elisha Niles	March 1, 1823	
Nehemiah Navens		
Nathan Noble		
Daniel Nickerson		
Goodman Noble	June 7, 1832	
John Norris		
Abraham Nott, or Knott	March 1, 1823	
Gamaliel Olmstead	June 7, 1832	
Daniel Olmstead	do.	
Isaac Ormsbee	do.	
Alexander Oliver	March 1, 1823	
Daniel O'Keiff	May 15, 1828	
Henry G. Ohlen	do.	
Mowbray Owen	do.	
John Ormsby		
Jonathan Owens	March 1, 1823	
John Phelps	June 7, 1832	
Ebenezer Plumley	do.	
Abel Porter	do.	
Ezekiel Pierce	do.	
Daniel Parke	do.	
James Parmele	do.	
Benjamin Pierce	do.	
James Powers	March 1, 1823	
Adoniram Parrot	do.	
Amable Paulent	May 15, 1828	
Charles Phillips	March 1, 1823	
Ebenezer Philips	do.	
Abiezer Perkins		
Eleazer Porter	do.	
Loring Peck	do.	
Chalker Pratt	do.	
Jesse Penfield	do.	
Cornelius Phelps	do.	
Benjamin Pettingill	do.	
Rufus Price		
James Parshall	May 15, 1828	
Ebenezer Patchin	March 1, 1823	
Sunderland Pattison	do.	
Ephraim Potter		
Salter Pulman	May 15, 1828	
Joseph Parks		
Thomas Plato		
William Parker, 1st		
Daniel Potter		
Richard J. Parker	do.	
Isaac Powers		
Jonathan Pratt	June 7, 1832	
Phineas Pond	May 15, 1828	
John Phillips, 3d	March 1, 1823	
Asa Porter		
Aaron Parks		
Zadock Pratt		
Joseph Porter		
Benjamin Palmer	do.	
David Peesley		
Samuel Petty	do.	

[Doc. No. 127.]
PENSIONERS IN NEW YORK—Continued.

Names.	Acts under which restored.	Remarks.
Jacob Rose		
Elmore Russell	June 7, 1832	
Preserved Redway	do.	
Abiezer Richmond	do.	
Josiah Rising	do.	
Samuel Round	do.	
Ziba Robinson	do.	
Daniel Roolo	do.	
Ensign Rexford	do.	
John Rynehart	March 1, 1823	
Robert Ryan	May 15, 1828	
Rufus Richardson	June 7, 1832	
Timothy Rossetter	March 1, 1823	
Frederick Ruford	do.	
Seth Rowley, 1st	do.	
John Rockwell		
Noah Roberts	do.	
Stephen Reed	do.	
Nathan Roberts		
John Royall	do.	
Joseph Reed, 2d	do.	
George Reab		
Bryan Rossetter	May 15, 1828	
Richard Risley	March 1, 1823	
Simeon Robertson		
Ebenezer Rogers	do.	
Edward Richmond		
John Rynders		
Lemuel Raymond		
Elisha Rose		
Stephen Risley	March 1, 1823	
Nathaniel Roberts	June 7, 1832	
Jacob Redington	May 20, 1830	
John Rice		
Elijah Risley	March 1, 1823	
Thomas Rankin	May 15, 1828	
Abner Rawson	March 1, 1823	
Tibbits Rathbone		
Jeremiah Rood		
David Rumsey	do.	
Thomas Spencer	do.	Relinquished for an increase of his stipend under the act of June 7, 1832.
Benjamin Stone	June 7, 1832	
Beriah Stiles	do.	
David Steele	do.	
John Strong	do.	
William Stephens	do.	
Enoch Story	do.	
Gideon Savage	do.	
Asher Saxton	do.	
John Snider	do.	
Aaron Sturgis	do.	
Ezekiel Scott	do.	
Ebenezer Still	do.	
John Shaw		
Robert Seaver	March 1, 1823	
Ebenezer Smith, 3d	do.	
William Shaw	do.	
Elihu Shelden	do.	
Gershom Sylvester	do.	
Job Snell		
Ezra Sibley	do.	

PENSIONERS IN NEW YORK—Continued.

Names.	Acts under which restored.	Remarks.
Peter Sitts	March 1, 1823	
Joseph Seymour		
John Stafford	do.	
Jonathan Sodon	do.	
Samuel Stowell	do.	
Zebulon Scriven		
Daniel Shields	May 15, 1828	
John Sutton		
Isaac Smith, 2d		
George Sinclair		
Samuel Stone		
Beriah Skinner		
James Selkirk		
Benjamin Swetland		
John St. John	Invalid.	Restored to invalid roll under the 3d section of the act of May 1, 1820: again placed on rev. roll under the act of March 1, 1823.
William Stocker	May 15, 1828	
Andrew Slowter	March 1, 1823	
David Southwick	May 15, 1828	
Stephen Smith	March 1, 1823	
Samuel Stebbins	do.	Relinquished for an increase of his stipend under the act of June 7, 1832.
Jacob Sax		
James Shields		
Ephraim Stone		
Ebenezer Storer	May 15, 1828	
George Sheaf		
Asa Squire	March 1, 1823	
Edward Spaulding	do.	
Samuel Stow		
Levi Stedman		
Isaac Smith		
Reuben Stickney		
James Stephenson	do.	
Hezekiah Smith	do.	
Nicholas Schuyler		
Moses Scott	May 15, 1828	
Oliver Stanard	do.	
Enos Scofield		
James Stephens	do.	
Ebenezer Smith	March 1, 1823	
William Shute	do.	
David Smith		
James Sanford		
Samuel Taylor, 1st	-	In these cases the pensioners never exhibited schedules of their property; but they were dropped because the department was informed that they were not in needy circumstances.
Nathan Taylor, 2d	-	
James Thompson, 3d	June 7, 1832	
Nathan Thompson	do.	
Jared Tuttle	do.	
Samuel Thomas	do.	
John Taylor, 2d	do.	
Zoeth Tucker	do.	
Samuel Tucker	March 1, 1823	
James Thompson, 2d	do.	
David Thorp	do.	
Zebulon Thompson	do.	
Joel Tuttle	do.	
Henry Dow Tripp		

[Doc. No. 127.]

PENSIONERS IN NEW YORK—Continued.

Names.	Acts under which restored.	Remarks.
Henry Thorn	March 1, 1823	
Stephen Thompson	May 15, 1828	
Calvin Tripp	March 1, 1823	
William Tabor	do.	
Samuel Thomas	June 7, 1832	
Hezekiah Tuttle	March 1, 1823	
Peter Tappen		
Peter Turner	May 15, 1828	
Lemuel Tingley	March 1, 1823	
Simeon Taylor		
James Thompson, 1st		
William Torrey	May 15, 1828	
Henry Thomas	do.	
James Thompson, 4th	March 1, 1823	
Joseph Tinkham		
Charles Turner	do.	
Stephen Toms		
Nathaniel Turner	do.	
Adam Trout		
Zachariah Tiffany		
Medad Taylor		
John Usher		
Joshua Vincent	June 7, 1832	
John Vanmater	March 1, 1823	
Ebenezer Vining	do.	
Henry Van Clarke		
Matthew Vanderpool		
John Van Horn		
John Van De Bogert		
Nicholas Van Rensselaer	May 15, 1828	
John Van Dyke	do.	
Joshua Whitney	June 7, 1832	
Benjamin Wright	do.	
John Wood, 2d	do.	
Samuel Wood	do.	
Joseph Williams	do.	
James Woodward	do.	
Benjamin White	do.	
Solomon Wood	do.	
Tobias Weygant	do.	
Caleb Willis	do.	
Nathan Williams	do.	
John Warren, 2d	do.	
John Watson, alias James Watson	May 15, 1828	
Shubael Welton	March 1, 1823	
William White, 3d	do.	
Joshua Webster	do.	
Josiah Wilcox	May 15, 1828	
Gad Warriner	March 1, 1823	
George Wright		
Lemuel Wheeler	do.	
Joseph Webb	do.	
Bazaliel Wright		
Sylvester Woodman	May 15, 1828	
Peter Wormwood	March 1, 1823	
Uriah Williams	do.	
Luke Woodbury	do.	
Dennison Wheedon	do.	
Benjamin Wells	do.	Relinquished for an increase of his stipend under the act of May 15, 1828.
William Whitehead	do.	

[Doc. No. 127.] 71

PENSIONERS IN NEW YORK—Continued.

Names.	Acts under which restored.	Remarks.
John Williams	May 15, 1828	
John Ward	do.	
John Wright, 1st		
John Ward, 2d		
Silas Wellman		
John Wandell	March 1, 1823	
John Watts		
Esek Whipple	do.	
Amos Whipley	May 15, 1828	
Ebenezer Whiting	March 1, 1823	
William Warren	May 15, 1828	
David Wheeler		
Aaron Warrener		
Asa Way	March 1, 1823	Relinquished for an increase of his stipend under the act of June 7, 1832.
Lemuel Wilcox	May 15, 1828	
John Wilson, 2d	March 1, 1823	
William Wallace	Invalid	Restored to invalid roll under the 3d section of the act of May 1, 1820: again placed on roll under the act of May 15, 1828.
Nathaniel White		
James R. Whitney		
Simeon Walling		
John Wolcott	March 1, 1823	
Christian Wallasie, alias Waliser		
David Wattles	do.	
Luther Washburn	do.	
Benjamin Waterous	do.	
John Wells		
James Wagon	do.	
Uriah White		
John Wright		
Gilbert Watkins		
Samuel Wolcott	do.	
Calvin Waterman	do.	
Jedediah Waterman	May 15, 1828	
Nathan Walden	March 1, 1823	
John Weatherstine, or Witderstein	May 15, 1828	
Giles Wolcott		
Gedor Woodruff	June 7, 1832	
Asa Wilkins	May 20, 1828	
Alexander Young		

72 [Doc. No. 127.]

PENSIONERS in New Jersey who have been dropped from the pension roll under the act of May 1st, 1820, prepared in conformity with the resolution of the House of Representatives of the 17th Dec. 1835.

Names.	Acts under which restored.	Remarks.
Joseph Applegate		
John Allen	– – – –	In this case the pensioner never exhibited a schedule of property; but his pension was stopped because the departm't was informed that he was not in needy circumstances.
James Array		
Samuel Allen, 2d		
Robert Applegate		
David Baker	– – June 7, 1832	
John Burroughs		
John Bolton		
Matthias Bowden or Boten		
James Burch		
Peter Brokaw		
James Bell		
Ezra Brown	– – March 1, 1823	
John Berry	– – do.	
Daniel Brown		
Samuel Bennett	– – do.	
Almarin Brooks	– – do.	
James Condon		
James Chambers	– – May 15, 1828	
Daniel Carty		
Abel Corson		
Daniel Cockrem		
Jabez Campfield		
Abner Condict	– – June 7, 1832	
Jacob Callater	– – March 1, 1823	
Daniel Congleton		
Bergun Covert	– – June 7, 1832	
James Collins		
John Chambers		
Squire Cockrem		
Cornelius Drake	– . March 1, 1823	
James Donaldson		
Enoch Durham	– – do.	
William Danbury	– – do.	
William Emberson		
Richard Edsall		
George Emmel	– – do.	
William Fulkerton		
Michael Fleming	– – do.	
William Fulper	– – do.	
Jonah Garrison	– – do.	
Bennet Garrison		
Mathias Garrison	– – do.	
Pierson Green		
Benjamin Guynip		
John Heard		
Barent Hartwick		
John Hoagland		
Joseph Hedges		
Hosea Husted		
Samuel Hicks	– – do.	
David Hubbs		
Benjamin Hamilton		
Reuben Husted	– – do.	
John Hopper		
David Hurd	– – do.	
ames Johnson, 1st		

[Doc. No. 127.] 73

PENSIONERS IN NEW JERSEY—Continued.

Names.	Acts under which restored.	Remarks.
Giles Jones		
James Johnson, 2d	March 1, 1823	
George Johnson		
William Johnson, 2d		
Henry Johnson	do.	
William Jewell		
John Kinney	do.	
Caleb Kimble		
Anthony King	May 15, 1828	
Sheppard Kollock	March 1, 1823	Relinquished for an increase of his stipend, under the act of June 7, 1832.
William Kelly		
Jacob Lippencut		
Thomas Lawrence	March 1, 1823	
Zenas Loder	do.	
Jacob Lacey		
Thomas Lamson	June 7, 1832	
Benoni Little		
Samuel Leonard	Invalid	Restored under 3d section, act May 1, 1820.
Randel McDuffey		
Cornelius Mills	March 1, 1823	
Ambrose Markham		
John Manning	do.	
John McKinney		
James McCaffery		
Edward Mills		
Usal Munson	do.	
Reuben Mosher		
Usal Micker	May 15, 1828	
William McKean	March 1, 1823	
Thomas Malaby	do.	
Garret Nevins	do.	
Benjamin Norman	June 7, 1832	
Jonathan Nicholas	May 15, 1828	
Lewis Nowe	March 1, 1823	
Darby Oram	June 7, 1832	
John Oakly		
Joseph Pangborn		
Rice Price		
Silas Parrot		
Joseph Pardoe		
Henry Post, 2d		
John Powers	March 1, 1823	
Thomas Perry		
James Raymond		
John Ryon		
James Rogers	do.	
Charles Stewart		
Josiah Steele	May 15, 1828	
William Stives	March 1, 1823	
William Stilwell		
James Smith	do.	
Isaac Sherman		
David Sickle, alias Van Sickle		
John Sandford	May 15, 1828	
Robert Stewart, (cook)		
James Stout		
Peter Sutton		
Valentine Sillcocks	- - -	In this case the pensioner never exhibited a schedule of his property; but his pension was stopped because the dep't was inform ed that he was not in needy circumstances.

PENSIONERS IN NEW JERSEY—Continued.

Names.	Acts under which restored.	Remarks.
John Sithins	March 1, 1823	
Asa Thomas	May 15, 1828	
James Throckmorton	June 7, 1832	
Holmes Throckmorton		
Abraham Tucker		
Amos Tompkins		
William Turner	March 1, 1823	
Caleb Tuttle	June 7, 1832	
James Toner	March 1, 1823	
Lemuel Tingley	do.	
Albert Voorheis	do.	
John Wilson		
Garret Williamson		
Ephraim Whitlock	do.	
John C. Willing		
Henry Waters		
Noadiah Wade		In this case the pensioner never exhibited a schedule of his property; but his pension was stopped because the department was informed that he was not in needy circumstances.
William Worth		
Samuel Wilkinson	March 1, 1823	
Robert Willson		
Isaac Williams		
James Willcock	June 7, 1832	
John Witz		
Peter Welch	March 1, 1823	

[Doc. No. 127.] 75

PENSIONERS in Pennsylvania who have been dropped from the pension roll under the act of 1st *of May,* 1820 ; *prepared in conformity with the resolution of the House of Representatives of the United States of the* 17th *of December,* 1835.

Names.	Acts under which restored.	Remarks.
William Amberson	May 15, 1828	
John Arthur	March 1, 1823	
Robert Barkley	June 7, 1832	
Jacob Bower		
Rufus Bennett	May 15, 1828	
Daniel Bowen	June 7, 1832	
Isaac Berlin	March 1, 1823	
Benoni Bates		
John Brown		
William Bargenhoff		
Jeremiah Bannon	March 1, 1823	
George Buyers	do.	
Stephen Bennett		
William Blake		
James Brown, 2d	May 15, 1828	
William Butler	March 1, 1823	
Benjamin Burd	do.	
Ebenezer Beeman	do.	
John Bernard		
John Baylie	June 7, 1832	
Daniel Bernhart	May 15, 1828	
Thomas Bowland		
Benjamin Bidlock	March 1, 1823	
Charles Bison or Bisson	do.	
Ebenezer Bartlett	do.	
George Beaver	do.	
Abner Blanchard		
John Battin		
Thomas Bevington	do.	
Joseph Britton	do.	
Isaac Brownson	do.	
William Branch	do.	
Selden Borden	do.	
Darius Calkins		
Thomas Craig	do.	Relinquished for an increase of his stipend under the act of the 15th May, 1828.
John Cosper		
John Collins	do.	
Nicholas Conly	do.	
Eli Catlin		
Casper Camp	do.	
John Clark, 4th		
Samuel Calender		
Jacob Cramer	May 20, 1830	
John Clark, 5th		
Joel Cook	June 7, 1832	
John Churchfield		
James Crutchlow	do.	
Richard Cheyney	March 1, 1823	
Leonard Corl	May 20, 1830	
George Cooper		
Benjamin Clark	May 15, 1828	
George Conner, sen.		
Henry Curtis or Henry Bass		
William Carson		
John Callender		
James Dixon		
John Dover		

PENSIONERS IN PENNSYLVANIA—Continued.

Names.	Acts under which restored.	Remarks.
Daniel Deiley		
Michael Dolin		
John Daly		
Michael Dodson		
Leonard Devons	June 7, 1832	
Daniel Davis	March 1, 1823	
William Dougherty	June 7, 1832	
Henry Doll	May 20, 1830	
Martin Doll		
Ludwig Dorman		
Dennis Dailly	March 1, 1823	
Patrick Dixson		
George R. Everson		
Edward Edgerton		
Arthur Eckles		
William Ferrell	do.	
Jacob Fetzer		
John Faust		
William Forbes		
Peter Fleck	do.	
Consider Fuller		
Daniel French, 2d		
William Farnshild	do.	
Jonathan Fowler	do.	
Michael Ferrick		
David Forrest	do.	
David Fox	do.	
Peter Fricker	do.	
Andrew Fox	do.	
Thomas Ford		
Isaac Franks		
Daniel Finly		
Philip Fry	do.	
George Godfrey, alias Felker		
Israel Greenleaf		
Ambrose Gaylord	May 15, 1828	
Hugh Gowan		
Daniel Graham		
James Greenland		
Alexander Graydon		
William George		
George Gangwoir	June 7, 1832	
Abraham Greenwolt		
Samuel D. Goff		
Joshua Griffin	May 15, 1828	
John Gunnell	March 1, 1823	
Adam Gramlin	June 7, 1832	
Obadiah Gore		
James Hagerman		
Thomas Hamilton	March 1, 1823	
Valentine Horse		
Leonard Hanse		
George House		
John Hoge	June 7, 1832	
Thomas Holland		
Jacob Holden		
Peter Heblinger		
William Henderson		
Adam Harboll		
James Hamilton		
John Heminger		
Henry Hilger		

[Doc. No. 127.] 77

PENSIONERS IN PENNSYLVANIA—Continued.

Names.	Acts under which restored.	Remarks.
Francis Harbison		
George Heiber	June 7, 1832	
Henry Hummel		
George Huber		
Jacob Hoff	March 1, 1823	
John Jamieson	do.	
Jacob Justice	May 15, 1828	
James Jacobs	March 1, 1823	
Joel Jones	do.	
James Josiah		
Benjamin Johnson	do.	
James Kelly		
Philip Krug, or Krugh		
George Kibber	do.	
Robert King		
Alexander King	do.	
John Keemle	do.	
Henry Klunck, or Clung	do.	
Michael Kuhns	June 7, 1832	
Adam Kock	March 1, 1823	
William Kerr	do.	
George Kersteller		
Anthon., Lehman		
Jehu Lewis	June 7, 1832	
Mungo Lindsey		
George Lucas	May 20, 1830	
Joseph Linebock		
John Loyd		
Hartman Lathiser	March 1, 1823	
Joseph Ledyard, sen.		
Daniel Leany		
William Leary		
David Lindsey	do.	
Amos Lawrence	May 15, 1828	
William Leard		
Nicholas Leib		
Laban Landon	do.	
William Magaw	do.	
Clement Masters		
Conrad Myers	June 7, 1832	
John Miller, 1st		
John McKeowen		
Edward McMasters	March 1, 1823	
John Michall		
George Morris	do.	
Peter McBride		
Enoch Morgan		
Alexander Martin		
John Manan	June 7, 1832	
William Martin		
Conrad Miller		
John Marshall		
Daniel McCarty	March 1, 1823	
John Martin	do.	
David Marshall		
John Montgomery	May 15, 1828	
John Moart	March 1, 1823	
Ahnond Munson	do.	
Isaac Morley		
Samuel Mellon		
John McClelland		
John Melone	May 15, 1828	

PENSIONERS IN PENNSYLVANIA—Continued.

Names.	Acts under which restored.	Remarks.
Thomas Murray		
Jacob Moyer, 2d		
Jacob Marks		
Philip Means	June 7, 1832	
David McCollom	March 1, 1823	
David Maffett	do.	
James McKinzey		
Henry Miller		
Reuben Mickle	do.	Relinquished for an increase of his stipend under the act of the 15th of May, 1828.
Martin Miller	March 3, 1831	Special act.
Alexander Moore		
Andrew Moore		
Robert McDonald	March 1, 1823	
John Nicholson		
James Norton		
Frederick Nipple	June 7, 1832	
Samuel Orsburne		
Murty O'Dorner		
Adam Oury	do.	
Dedrick Ourhand		
Michael Peter		
George Preise		
Henry Pennsinger		
Comfort Peters	March 1, 1823	
Jared Phelps	do.	
John Patridge	do.	
James Parsons		
Frederick Rively		
David Ramsay		
Conrad Rimee		
Thomas Ryerson	do.	
Isaac Rosebrough	do.	
William Russell	do.	
Abraham Rinker		
Philip M. Russell	do.	
Benedict Reynolds	June 7, 1832	
Stephen Roberts		
James Ryburn		
Zephaniah Rogers		
George Rees	March 1, 1823	
Isaac Rynearson	do.	
Samuel Rutan	June 7, 1832	
James Reed		
Daniel St. Clair	May 15, 1828	
Peter Shumway	do.	
George S. Searls	March 1, 1823	
Moses Smith		
Adam Stall		
Andrew Sax	do.	
Edward Smith		
John Smith, 2d		
Daniel Salliday, or Salloday		
Samuel C. Seely		
Philip Peter Schriver		
Elijah Starr		
Michael Spatz	June 7, 1832	
Ebenezer Seeley	do.	
James Smith, 2d		
Roger Stayner	March 1, 1823	Relinquished for an increase of his stipend under the act of the 15th of May, 1828.
Matthias Shroyer		

PENSIONERS IN PENNSYLVANIA—Continued.

Names.	Acts under which restored.	Remarks.
John Spires		
Robert Shandler		
Joseph Smith	May 15, 1828	
Elisha Satterlee	March 1, 1823	
Ichabod Seaver	do.	
John Sims		
John Smith, 4th	June 7, 1832	
John Spalding		
Stephen Sparrow	March 1, 1823	
John Schneider		
David Shearer	do.	
Nathaniel Stevenson	do.	
Lemuel Standlief	June 7, 1832	
William Southworth	March 1, 1823	
George Trine	June 7, 1832	
Thomas Turner		
John Tiffany		
Joseph Thomas	March 1, 1823	
James Thayer	June 7, 1832	
Andrew Tryer		
William Taylor, 2d	do.	
Solon Trescott		
William Tindall	March 1, 1823	
John Verner	May 15, 1828	
Benjamin Wheeler	do	
Andrew Wilson	March 1, 1823	
George Wiseman	do.	
John Wort	June 7, 1832	
Samuel Whitehead		
John Wilson		
Edward Woodman		
James Winters		
Henry Weaver	March 1, 1823	
Joseph Welsh		
Benjamin Watson	May 15, 1828	
John B. Webster	March 1, 1823	Relinquished for an increase of his stipend under the act of the 15th of May, 1828.
Frederick Willhelm		
Frederick William Wock		
Joseph Williams		
Ichabod Ward	do.	
Jacob Wisner	do.	
John Witz	June 7, 1832	
John Welsh	March 1, 1823	
John Youse		

PENSIONERS *in Delaware who have been dropped from the pension roll under the act of the 1st of May,* 1820, *prepared in conformity with the resolution of the House of Representatives of the United States, of the 17th of December,* 1835.

Names.	Acts under which restored.	Remarks.
Bartholomew Adams		
Caleb P. Bennett	May 15, 1828	
Jacob Creamer		
John Corse		
Whitenton Clifton		
Frazier Gray	March 1, 1823	
David Kirkpatrick	do.	Relinquished for an increase of his stipend under the act of May 15, 1828.
John Marks		
Stayton Morris		
Joab Polk		
Edward Roche		
Zachariah Rossell	do.	

[Doc. No. 127.] 81

PENSIONERS in the State of Maryland who have been dropped from the pension roll under the act of May 1, 1820; prepared in conformity with the resolution of the House of Representatives of the 17th of December, 1835.

Names.	Acts under which restored.	Remarks.
William Bruce		
Ignatius Brashears	June 7, 1832	
Benjamin Boyd		
Robert Boxwell		
Vachel Burgess		
Joseph Boxwell	March 1, 1823	
John Carr		
William Coe	June 7, 1832	
Hugh Cane		
Andrew Craven		
James Chambers	March 1, 1823	
Jacob Collins		
Thomas Carney	do.	
James Davidson	June 7, 1832	
Edward Dickenson		
Benjamin Duvall		
Anthony Davis		
George Dent		
John Eisell	March 1, 1823	
James Ervin	do.	
Emanuel Ebbs		
Wolfgang Eichberger		
James Fling	June 7, 1832	
John Franks		
John Fossett		
Edward B Goddard		
Samuel Griffeth	do.	
Gabriel Galworth	do.	
Joseph Hook	do.	
Jesse Hoshal		
Peter Hammond		
Lazarus Harman	May 15, 1828	
John Hawkins Hays		
Archibald Johnson		
Philip Jones		
Michael Kerchner		
Thomas Lynch	March 1, 1823	
Henry Leeke		
William Layman	do.	
Edward Mahony		
John McCauley		
James McCracken	do.	
Thomas McKeel		
Charles Oldwine	do.	
Adam Ott	do.	
Thomas Pamphillion		
James Ramsey		
Joshua Rutledge		
Richard Stevens		
Levi Stevens	June 7, 1832	
John Shryock	March 1, 1823	
Henry Spaulding	do.	
John Smith, 2d		
Jesse Thompson	May 15, 1828	
George Vaughn	Invalid	Restored under the 3d section of the act of the 1st May, 1820.
Gassaway Watkins	May 15, 1828	
Frederick Wilhied	March 1, 1823	
Benjamin Young		

PENSIONERS *in the District of Columbia who have been dropped from the pension roll under the act of* 1*st May,* 1820; *prepared in conformity with the resolution of the House of Representatives of the* 17*th December,* 1835.

Names.	Acts under which restored.	Remarks.
Hugh Barr		
John Barker		
Robert Brown		
Richard Coe	June 7, 1832	
Andrew Cutler		
Zephaniah Terrill		
Richard Fenwick	March 1, 1823	
Joseph Fearson		
Francis Hagins		
Thomas Jenkins	June 7, 1832	
John Philips	March 1, 1823.	
Clement Sewell	Invalid	Restored under the 3d section of the act of 1st May, 1820. Also on the roll under the act of May 15, 1828.
Joseph Wheaton	March 1, 1823	Relinquished for an increase of his stipend under the act of May 15, 1828.

[Doc. No. 127.]   83

PENSIONERS in the State of Virginia who have been dropped from the pension roll under the act of the 1st *May,* 1820 ; *prepared in conformity with the resolution of the House of Representatives of the* 17th *December,* 1835.

Names.	Acts under which restored.	Remarks.
John Arundale		
Jonathan Adams	May 15, 1828	
Thomas Athy		
John Bryant		
William Bunting		
John Beasley		
Ezekiel Burrows		
Aaron Ball		
George Brook		
William Bentley		
John C. Blatchford		
Aaron Belvin		
Benjamin Barham		
Charles Barrage		
Francis Burch		
Pleasant Bybee	March 1, 1823	
Richard Bangham		
James Berry		
Henry Buckhannon	do.	
Samuel B. Bell	do.	
Abraham Burner		
Gustavus Croston	May 15, 1828	
Robert Chambers	June 7, 1832	
Benjamin Chesney	May 15, 1828	
Thomas Carter		
Stephen Cheatham		
Anthony Coon	June 7, 1832	
Benjamin Chappell		
Archibald Casey		
Parker Copes	March 1, 1823	
James Chenault		
John Collins		
Lewis Clark		
Thomas Coverly	Invalid	Restored under the 3d section of the act of the 1st May, 1820.
John Cole		
John Clarke	March 1, 1823	
Elijah Dickinson	do.	
Reuben Davenport		
Thomas Dix		
Peter Dagger		
Westbrook Day		
Thomas Daudeen		
Joshua Dunn		
Robert Dugar		
Benjamin Dawson		
Hugh Davis	do.	
John Ethrington	do.	
Thomas Elliott		
Newit Edwards	do.	
William Elliott		
Claiborn Elder		
Rowland Estes		
Nathaniel Fox		
William Forbes or Furbush		
Obadiah Fawcett		
George Forrest		
Joachim Fetzer		
Archibald Finley		
Patrick Gleason		

PENSIONERS IN VIRGINIA—Continued.

Names.	Acts under which restored.	Remarks.
Zachariah Goff		
John Greathouse	June 7, 1832	
Joseph Gilbert	March 1, 1823	
John Galleger	do.	
John Guthry	do.	
Benjamin Gallaway	do.	
William Grady	do.	
Elijah Green	do.	
John Hixon		
James Harris	do.	
Elisha Hobbs		
John Henderson		
Youst Heck		
Henry Hines	do.	
Francis Hughs		
Jacob Hoover	do.	
Ralph R. Horn		
Vincent Hudson		
Thomas Hale	do.	
Sampson Henderson		
John Holtz		
William Hix	June 7, 1832	
Robert Horton		
John Haydon		
John Hargrove		
Thomas Harris		
Bernard Houching		
John Harris, 4th	March 1, 1823	
Edward Haymond		
John Hackney	May 15, 1828	
John Harris, 5th		
Thomas Hood	March 1, 1823	
Jacob Hunt	do.	
Anselem Ivie		
John J. Jacob	May 15, 1828	
Richard Joy	Invalid	Restored under the 3d section of the act of the 1st May, 1820.
John Jordan	March 1, 1823	Relinquished for an increase of his stipend under the act of the 15th May, 1828.
Lewellin Jones		
Giles Johnson		
John Jones, 2d		
Samuel Johnson	March 1, 1823	
William Knight		
Aaron Lockart		
Walter Linsey		
Benoni Lipscomb		
Benjamin Lawson		
Christopher Loving		
Isaac Lucardo	June 7, 1832	
John Lipscomb		
William Lawrence		
Thomas Marsh		
George Murfree		
Austin Meeks		
John Maddox	May 15, 1828	
Peter Montague		
Andrew McCarty		
Martin Mooney	March 1, 1823	
Thomas Mitchell		
James Martin		
Charles Melson		

[Doc. No. 127.]   85

PENSIONERS IN VIRGINIA—Continued.

Names.	Acts under which restored.	Remarks.
William Moody, 2d		
Zadock Marris	May 15, 1828	
Jesse Moore	March 1, 1823	
John Morriss	do.,	
Lewis Miller	do.	
Abraham Maury	June 7, 1832	
Thomas McGee	March 1, 1823	
Henry H. Norvell	do.	
Thomas New		
John Newman	Invalid	Restored under the 3d section of the act of the 1st May, 1820.
James Oliver		
Erasmus Oakley		
Alexander Parker	March 1, 1823	
William Phillips	June 7, 1832	
John Phillips	March 1, 1823	
Moses Perry		
Thomas Plunkett	do.	
Joseph Parnett		
James Peters		
Jesse Pace		
Nusum Pace	June 7, 1832	
John Pierce		
Thomas Rowse		
Philip Richcreek		
Samuel Russel, 1st	March 1, 1823	
Robert Richardson	do.	
Hosea Rogers	do.	
Holliday Revel	June 7, 1832	
Robert Rutherford	March 1, 1823	
Richard Roberts	do.	
John Starkey		
James Smith, 1st		
Leonard Shackelford	June 7, 1832	
Joseph Smith		
Larkin Self		
Richard Shott		
George Suggs	March 1, 1823	
John Spinner		
John Smith, 5th		
Edward Sanford	do.	
John Smith, 6th		
Benjamin Strother	Invalid	Restored under the 3d section of the act of 1st May, 1820.
Michael Sword	June 7, 1832	
Thomas Shores, 1st	do.	
John Spitfathom	March 1, 1823	
John Spencer		
George Shaner	do.	
Peter Stivers	do.	
James Thompson		
William Talliaferro	June 7, 1832	
William Thornton		
Buckner Thomas		
Ferguson Taylor	May 15, 1828	
John Trezvant		
Smith Thompson	March 1, 1823	
Reuben Tucker		
Gideon Terry		
Vincent Tapp		
Peter Taff		

PENSIONERS IN VIRGINIA—Continued.

Names.	Acts under which restored.	Remarks.
Peter Triplett	March 1, 1823	
Jacob Wade		
John Wright, 2d	May 15, 1828	
Robert Watterson	March 1, 1823	
Henry Wymer		
William Wroe		
Isaac Welch		
John Williams		
Hugh Wallace	Invalid	Restored under 3d section of the act of the 1st May, 1820.

[Doc. No. 127.]   87

PENSIONERS in North Carolina who have been dropped from the pension roll under the act of May 1, 1820; *prepared in conformity with the resolution of the House of Representatives of the* 17*th December,* 1835.

Names.	Acts under which restored.	Remarks.
John Anderson	June 7, 1832	
John Artiss		
James Blackwell		
John Henry Blum		
Henry Barnhill	do.	
Stephen Bailey	March 1, 1823	
Charles Butler		
John Curry	June 7, 1832	
Jeremiah Crysel	March 1, 1823	
Solomon Carr		
Osborn Clark		
Isaac Clark	do.	
Samuel Chappel	do.	
Isaac Chapman		
Peter Douge		
George Dudley	do.	
Cyrus Davis	do.	
George Duncan	do.	
John Denton	do.	
Michael Ellis	June 7, 1832	
Edmund Foster	March 1, 1823	
Robert Faucett or Forcett		
Isham Finch		
David Fink		
William Gray		
Charles Gordon		
Nathan Gwaltney	do.	
Charles Gibson		
Samuel Gerock	do.	Relinquished for an increase of his stipend, under the act of June 7, 1832.
Jesse Harrison	do.	
Isaac Herrington	do.	
Ebenezer Hewett	May 15, 1828	
Daniel Hopkins		
James Johnson	March 1, 1823	
Brittain Jones	do.	
Hardy Jones		
Peter Jones	do.	
David King	June 7, 1832	
William Keene	March 1, 1823	
Joseph Lovett	do.	
John Lacy		
John Lambert		
Andrew Likens		
Thomas Love	do.	
Thomas Lee		
Reps Maybry		
Gilbert Matthews		
Dixon Marshall		
Hugh McDonald	do.	
Gardner Moy		
Jeremiah Munday	do.	
Joshua Martin		
Daniel McCleran		
Robert Martin	do.	
Simeon Moore		
William Morgan		
Giles Nelson	June 7, 1832	

[Doc. No. 127.]
PENSIONERS IN NORTH CAROLINA—Continued.

Names.	Acts under which restored.	Remarks.
James Overton	March 1, 1823	
Austin Prescott	May 15, 1828	
Isaac Perkens'	March 1, 1823	
David Poe		
Mitchell Phillips		
Willoughby Prescott	May 15, 1828	
Isaiah Parr		
Frederick Rigsby	March 1, 1823	
William Ryall	May 15, 1828	
John Rogerson		
John Rowan	March 1, 1823	
John Sexton	do.	
David Smith		
Jesse Shivers		
Seth Sterling	do.	
Valentine Shepperd	June 7, 1832	
Thomas Shute		
John Smith		
William Spain	do.	
John Stephens	March 1, 1823	
George Twiford	do.	
John Thomas		
Thomas Taunt		
James White		
William Warren		
John Womble		
William Wood	do.	
Benjamin Wheeler		
George Wallace	May 15, 1828	
James Woodland or Woolard		
James Wiley	March 1, 1823	

[Doc. No. 127.] 89

PENSIONERS in South Carolina, who have been dropped under the act of May 1, 1820; prepared in conformity with a resolution of the House of Representatives of the United States, of the 17th of December, 1835.

Names.	Acts under which restored.	Remarks.
William Ashley	March 1, 1823	
John Butler		
Samuel Bratcher		
Harmen Comens	June 7, 1832	
Martin Cole	March 1, 1823	
Ripley Copeland	June 7, 1832	
Peter Cherry	March 1, 1823	
Henry Cole	do.	
John Cook, 2d	do.	
Robert Cowley		
Thomas Cooper		
Charles Dick	do.	
Perry Evans	May 15, 1828	
Deason Enlow		
Johnson Elkins		
Philip Martin Frey		
Joshua Foster		
George St. George		
James Gassaway	March 1, 1823	
Thomas Gaines	do.	
George Gosling		
Hugh Houston	do.	
John Huffman	do.	
James Halks		
Pendleton Isbell		
Jacob Jones	June 7, 1832	
John King	do.	
Grant Knowlton		
Thomas Kolb		
Abraham Kelly	March 1, 1823	
James King		
Hugh Knox		
James Kirkpatrick		
Basil Lowe	May 15, 1828	
Blackman Ligan		
Andrew Melloy		
Richard McCary	March 1, 1823	
Martin Martin	do.	
James Motes	do.	
John Miller		
Aaron Odam		
Thomas Owens		
William Plant, sen.		
Needham Perrit		
George Petrie		
Levi Philips	do.	
Nicholas Rochester		
George Roebuck	June 7, 1832	
James Strange	March 1, 1823	
James Seay	June 7, 1832	
David Scott	do.	
James Stewart		
Moses Spivey	March 1, 1823	
John Smith	do.	
John Swords		
Edward Sims	May 15, 1828	
William Smith		
Isaac Smith		

PENSIONERS IN SOUTH CAROLINA—Continued.

Names.	Acts under which restored.	Remarks.
George Turner		
Jonathan Taylor		
Flanders Thompson	March 1, 1823	
Stephen Truhitt		
William Townsend	May 15, 1828	
John Wickley		
Henry Weaver	March 1, 1823	

[Doc. No. 127.] 91

PENSIONERS in Georgia, who have been dropped under the act of May 1, 1820; *prepared in conformity with a resolution of the House of Representatives of the United States, of the 17th of December,* 1835.

Names.	Acts under which restored.	Remarks.
David Ambrose		
William Beale		
William Bryant	March 1, 1823	
Daniel Clower	do.	
John Crosson	do.	
Joseph Curbow	June 7, 1832	
James Dillard	March 1, 1823	
Charles Garner	do.	
Thomas Grimsley	do.	
Thomas Howard	do.	
Joseph Payne Johnson	do.	
Abraham P. Jones	do.	
James Kelan	do.	
David Kerr		
Philip Logan		
John Martin	do.	
William Milirons		
Jesse Peters	June 7, 1832	
Jesse Ricketson	do.	
Richard Roberts		
Jacob Solter	March 1, 1823	
Austin Smith		
William Stephens	do.	
James Sutley	do.	
Edward Tenney		
James Tison		
John Talley		
William Willoughby		
Moses Wade		

PENSIONERS in the State of Alabama who have been dropped from the pension roll under the act of May 1, 1820; *prepared in conformity with the resolution of the House of Representatives of the 17th of December,* 1835.

Names.	Acts under which restored.	Remarks.
John Davis		
Jesse Dodd	March 1, 1823	
Benjamin French	do.	
James McIlheny		
Jesse Meredith	do.	
John Smith, 2d	June 7, 1832	
William Wagster	March 1, 1823	

[Doc. No. 127.]

PENSIONERS in Kentucky, who have been dropped from the pension roll under the act of the 1st May, 1820; prepared in conformity with the resolution of the House of Representatives of the 17th December, 1835.

Names.	Acts under which restored.	Remarks.
William Adams	March 1, 1823	Relinquished for an increase of his stipend, under the act of June 7, 1832.
William Alexander	do	
Barnabas Allen		
John Adams, 2d		
John Allen	June 7, 1832	
William Barker		
William Ballenger		
Solomon Belew		
Ambrose Barnett	do	
Zachariah Burch		
Nicholas Baker		
John Beatty	do	
James Brooks	March 1, 1823	
Charles Brown	do	
Obadiah Basshan	do	
Henry Brewer	do	
Thomas Berry	do	
Patin Brown	do	
Thomas Carothers		
James Carothers	do	
Matthew Cummings	do	Relinquished for an increase of his supend, under the act of June 7, 1832.
Sterling Crowder	June 7, 1832	
Goldsley Childers	do	
John Collett	March 1, 1823	
Richard Cains		
Obadiah Carter		
Isaac Coovert		
John Curd	do	
Thomas Coleman		
James Coghill		
Frederick Cooper		
Peter Demoss	June 7, 1832	
Thomas Davis, 1st	do	
Robert Downs		
John Ducker	do	
William Davis	May 15, 1828	
William Dale		
Francis Driver		
James Durham	March 1, 1823	
Andrew Dilman		
David Driskell	do	
Thomas Downing	do	
Samuel Dehart	do	
John Emmerson	do	Relinquished for an increase of his stipend, under the act of May 15, 1828.
John Edwards	May 15, 1828	
William Farmer		
Samuel Fate		
John Fleece	do	
William Foster		
Thomas Fitzsimmons	do	
William Ferguson	March 1, 1823	
John Finley	do	Relinquished for an increase of his stipend under act of May 15, 1828.
Charles Green		
Daniel Gano	do	Relinquished for an increase of his stipend, under the act of June 7, 1832.

[Doc. No. 127.] 93
PENSIONERS IN KENTUCKY—Continued.

Names.	Acts under which restored.	Remarks.
George Gray		
Samuel Gunison		
Job Garvey		
John Goatley	May 15, 1828	
Sikes Garris	June 7, 1832	
Benjamin Hardin	do	
John Humfres	do	
William Hampton		
Robert Hopkins		
John How	March 1, 1823	
Michael Hargan	June 7, 1832	
William Hubbell		
Hardy Hynes		
Philip Hammond		
Garner Hopkins	March 1, 1823	
Joseph James		
James Johnson, 1st	do	
Robert Johnson		
Samuel Jones	June 7, 1832	
Peter Jordan		
Benjamin Kendrick	Invalid	Restored under the 3d section of the act of 1st May, 1820.
William Kendrick	March 1, 1823	
William Kerns	June 7, 1832	
Robert Kirk	May 15, 1828	
Charles Love		
Hiram Mitchell		
William McIntire	March 1, 1823	
John Miles		
William Moffitt	do	
George Moxley		
William Miles		
James McCalley		
Robert Moseley		
James McCowan		
Alexander McLarde		
John Motthrop		
Alexander McPherson	March 1, 1823	
Mark McPherson	do	Relinquished for an increase of his stipend under act 15th May, 1828.
Larkin Minor		
John Miller		
Joshua McQueen	May 15, 1828	
John Mountjoy		
Gabriel Murphy		
Darby McGannon		
Benjamin Mann	March 1, 1823	
Alven Mountjoy		
William Margan	May 15, 1828	
John McMahon		
Thomas Murray	March 1, 1823	
James McGuire	June 7, 1832	
Daniel McCoy	March 1, 1823	
William Martin	do	
William Parish		
William Purvis	do	
John Patterson		
Mesheke Pearson	do	
Nathan Preston	do	
Moses Preston	do	
Jesse Puryear	do	
James Pritchett		

94 [Doc. No. 127.]

PENSIONERS IN KENTUCKY—Continued.

Names.	Acts under which restored.	Remarks.
Charles Pelham	March 1, 1823	
John Pollett	do.	
Thomas Ramsey	do.	
Hugh Rankin		
Jesse Rose		
Andrew Rogers	do.	
John Roberts		
Edward Roberts		
Jacob Rooksberry		
John Reed		
Zachariah Reed		
George Richards		
Thomas Ravenscraft		
James Rainey		
John Smith		
Richard Simms		
Joseph Sidebottom	March 1, 1823	
Seth Stratton	May 15, 1828	
William Sims	March 1, 1823	
Beane Smallwood	June 7, 1832	
John Stephens		
James Sherrell	do.	
Cudbeth Stone		
George Spindlebower	March 1, 1823	
John Sidebottom		
Jacob Stevens	do.	
Medley Shelton	do.	
John Snead	do.	
Aquilla Smith	Invalid	Restored under the 3d section of the act of 1st May, 1820.
Godfrey Smith		
Edward Stoker	March 1, 1823	
Elisha Thomas		
John J. Thomas	do.	
John Taylor		
John Tutwiler	do.	
Solomon Turner		
William Taylor	do.	Relinquished for an increase of his stipend under act 15th May, 1828.
Perry Tharp	May 15, 1828	
Lewis Thomas	do.	
William Thurman		
Charles Tyler	March 1, 1823	
William Turner	do.	
Joseph Vance		
Joseph Wilkinson	June 7, 1832	
Thaddeus H. Warmouth	March 1, 1823	
Raphael Winsett	do.	
Henry Wyatt		
Joshua Wayland		
Jacob Weatherholt	do.	
John Waller		
Thomas Wright	do.	
John Waldren		
John Williams	do.	
Bennett Williams	do.	
Ichabod Wheadon	do.	
Nathan Young		
Joshua York	do.	
Alexander Young	do.	

[Doc. No. 127.]   95

PENSIONERS in Ohio who have been dropped from the pension roll under the act of May 1, 1820; prepared in conformity with the resolution of the House of Representatives of the 17th December, 1835.

Names.	Acts under which restored.	Remarks.
Moses Adams	March 1, 1823	
Henry Aldred	do.	
Stephen Ames	do.	
John Burns		
Elijah Beardsley	do.	
Samuel Baskerville	do.	Relinquished for an increase of his stipend under the act of May 15, 1828.
William Bierce	do.	Relinquished for an increase of his stipend under the act of June 7, 1832.
John Barnes	do.	
Nicholas Bergerhoof	do.	
Thomas Beall		
Benjamin Blankinship	June 7, 1832	
Obiel or Obil Beach	do.	
John Bareth	May 15, 1828	
Humphrey Beckett	June 7, 1832	
Asa Benjamin		
Benjamin Barrett	March 1, 1823	
Jeremiah Burnham	do.	
Samuel Brown		
David Bay		
Ramoth Bunting	do.	
Jacob Bushong		
John Buck		
Henry Baumgarten	do.	
Azor Bagley	do.	
Michael Bowen	do.	
William Blunt		
Ebenezer Bostwick	May 15, 1828	
Stephen Butler		
Nathaniel Bettis	March 1, 1823	
Elijah Burroughs		
Stephen Baldwin		
John Blue		
Jacob Bower	do.	
Joseph Badger	do.	
John Barr		
James Blackburn	do.	
James Bonwell		
Thomas Cunningham		
Roswell Cawkins		
Johnson Cook	Invalid	Restored to invalid roll under 3d section of act of May 1, 1820; again restored under act of March 1, 1823.
Roswell Cook		
Philip Connor		
Samuel Carson		
Patrick Cunningham	March 1, 1823	
Andrew Cypruss	May 15, 1828	
Gideon Crittenden	March 1, 1823	
William Cart	do.	
Christopher Colson		
William Chambers		
John Clark		
John Camp	June 7, 1832	
Michael Curts		
Zerah Curtiss	March 1, 1823	
Henry Cherry		
Abner Cochrane		

PENSIONERS IN OHIO—Continued.

Names.	Acts under which restored.	Remarks.
James Curry		
Phineas Coburn - -	June 7, 1832	
Thomas Corey		
Elijah Canfield		
William Dixon - -	March 1, 1823	
Elias Daily		
Thomas Dickerson		
Richard Done		
Jonathan Davis - -	do.	
James Devon or Devaun		
Gideon Daggett - -	do.	
Stephen Dunwell - -	June 7, 1832	
Ephraim Ellis - -	do.	
Jonathan Emerson		
Jacob Ettinger - -	March 1, 1823	
Joseph L. Finley - -	do.	Relinquished for an increase of his stipend under the act of the 15th May, 1828.
Valentine Fritts		
Caleb Fowler		
Parker Fellowes		
Joseph Fuller - -	May 15, 1828	
Luther Frisbie - -	do.	
George Francis		
Job Foster - -	June 7, 1832	
William Fuller - -	March 1, 1823	
Amos Gustin		
Arthur Gillis		
George Gwinup - -	May 15, 1828	
Thadeus Gilbert - -	March 1, 1823	
William Gates - -	do.	
John H. Goodrich		
Ebenezer Goss - -	do.	
Eleazer Gillson - -	May 15, 1828	
John Green - -	March 1, 1823	
Charles Hamilton		
Thomas Hammond		
Levi Hamblin		
Thomas Haley - -	do.	
Evan Holt - -	May 15, 1828	
Elisha Hinsdale - -	March 1, 1823	
Arthur Hazzard		
Sylvanus Hulet		
David Hickock		
Robert Hunter		
Robert Hamilton - -	May 15, 1828	
Moses Haskill		
Amasa Howe		
Richard Hardin		
Nathan Hollister - -	June 7, 1832	
Durbin Hickock		
Solomon Jones		
Joseph Jackson		
Henry Jolly - -	March 1, 1823	
Benjamin Johnson		
Philemon Kirkum		
Francis Kelsimere - -	do.	
Andrew Kennedy		
Jared Kimball - -	do.	
Alex'r Kingman or Kingram	do.	
Joseph Lummis - -	do.	
James Landon or Langdon -	do.	
Patrick Logan		

[Doc. No. 127.]

PENSIONERS IN OHIO—Continued.

Names.	Acts under which restored.	Remarks.
Henry Loar		
Abraham Lyon		
Frederick Loveland	March 1, 1823	
Thomas Mason	do	
Samuel Mansfield		
William Manlove		
Levi Munsell	June 7, 1832	
Connelly McFaden	March 1, 1823	
John McKnight	do	
Robert McCullough		
Peter Magee		
William Matthews	do	
Redmont McDonough		
Jonathan Mansfield	do	
William McGee	do	
Felix McIlhany	do	
James Moore	do	
William Norris	June 7, 1832	
Joseph Osborn	March 1, 1823	
Benjamin Page	June 7, 1832	
Jonathan Parker		
Elias Pegg	March 1, 1823	
Joseph Price	do	
David Pierson		
Daniel Pierson		
John Potts		
John Palmer		
Joel Philbrook		
Benjamin Prichard		
David Preston		
Abijal Perry		
Mathias Pearson	May 15, 1828	
Samuel Pierson	do	
William Pelham		
Ichabod Pomeroy	June 7, 1832	
Michael Parks	do	
John Reynolds	March 1, 1823	
William Rhodes	Invalid	Restored under 3d section act May 1, 1820.
James Reilly	June 7, 1832	
Thomas Ratton	do	
Aaron Ruse	do	
William Rogers	March 1, 1823	
Daniel Rankins	do	
James Richards		
Mathias Rail, or Roll		
Robert Rickey		
Oliver Robinson	do	
Justus Reynolds	do	
Lemuel Rucker	do	
James Rusk	do	
Charles Rounes	do	
Daniel Reddington		
Benjamin Rice, or Rue		
Oliver Rice	May 15, 1828	
Jacob Rose	do	
Jonathan Swett	March 1, 1823	
John Simonton	do	
Beverly Spencer		
Jesse Swem	do	
Mathias Shirtz	do	
Silvanus Smith		
Jonathan Smith	May 15, 1828	
John Smith		

PENSIONERS IN OHIO—Continued.

Names.	Acts under which restored.	Remarks.
Amos Stackhouse		
William Smith, 4th	March 1, 1823	
Lemuel Snow		
James Swinnerton		
Timothy Smith, 1st	March 1, 1823	
Josiah Simpson	do	
Henry Smith		
Jacob Shaffer		
James Sprague	do	
Thomas Simpson		
Thomas Stothard		
John Seley	May 15, 1828	
John Seward		
Nicholas Siprill		
Caspar Stoner		
Andrew Shaffer		Harmon's regiment, Pennsylvania line.
Andrew Shaffer	June 7, 1832	Ganby's regiment, Maryland line.
Timothy Sherman		
Phineas Shepperd	do	
Skeen Douglass Sackett	do	
John Shaw		
Thomas Stannage	do	
George Spickard	March 1, 1823	Relinquished for an increase of his stipend under the act of June 7, 1832.
John Thompson		
John Tuttle.		
Seth Thompson	do	
John Tellis, sen.		
John Trotler	do	
James Terney		
James Tucker	do	
William Taylor	do	
John Turner		
Daniel Tyler	do	
Richard Talbot		
Merifield Vicory	do	
George Vannostran		
Peter Walker	do	
Reuben M. Wilder	do	
Ezekiel Woodworth	do	
Thomas Woods	do	
Ebenezer Wood	do	
Jonathan Wood	June 7, 1832	
John Williams, 1st.		
James Walters	March 1, 1823	
George Weightman	do	
Joseph Witter		
Timothy Wells		
Peter Wyrick		
John Walters		
Christopher Walter	May 15, 1828	
Meshec Walker	do	
Israel Wells		
James Williams	March 1, 1823	
Amos Wheeler		
William Wilson		
Ichabod Wilkinson		
Edward Warren	Invalid	Restored under 3d section act May 1, 1820.
Andrew Webster	June 7, 1832	
Peter Walters		
William White	March 1, 1823	
William Wardwell	do	
John Wheeler	do	
Michael Zane, or Sayner		

[Doc. No. 127.] 99

PENSIONERS in Tennessee who have been dropped under the act of May 1, 1820; *prepared in conformity with a resolution of the House of Representatives of the United States of the 17th of December,* 1835.

Names.	Acts under which restored.	Remarks.
Moses Allen	June 7, 1832	
James Blackburn		
Philip Britain	March 1, 1823	
Jesse Bryant		
David E. Brown	do.	
Lance James Barnett		
Isham Brown		
Joseph Britton	do.	Relinquished for an increase of his stipend under the act of May 15, 1828.
James Baggett	do.	
Squire Baker		
David Benton		
Edward Brus, alias Banks		
Andrew Bay	June 7, 1832	
Joshua Curtis		
Sylvester Chum	March 1, 1823	
John Carney	do.	
Benjamin Crab	do.	
James Crews	do.	
Michael Courtney	do.	
Alexander Downie		
Nicholas Davis	do.	
John Doyle	do.	
David Dodd	do.	
Samuel Davis	do.	
James Davis		
Farrel O'Neil Daily		
William Douglass	-	In this case the pensioner never exhibited a schedule of his property; but his pension was stopped because the department was informed that he was not in needy circumstances.
Robert Everitt		
Richard Eppes		
Joseph Evans	do.	
Henry Franklin		
Jonathan Faire	do.	
Thomas Gamble		
Thomas Gilbreath	do.	
Joel Gunter	do.	
John Gibson	do.	
John Harbison		
Gideon Hogh	do.	
Stephen Handlin		
John Hall		
Isaac Horton	do.	
Thomas Harper	do.	
Michael Ingle		
Elisha E. Johnson		
Benjamin Johnson		
Edward King	May 15, 1828	
William Keeble	March 1, 1823	
Joseph Lemaster	do.	
John Lasley	do.	
William Lumbley	do.	
Michael Menably, alias McNelly		
William Mackey	do.	

PENSIONERS IN TENNESSEE—Continued.

Names.	Acts under which restored.	Remarks.
John Merris		
John McCullock	March 1, 1823	
James Morriston	June 7, 1832	
John McCalla	March 1, 1823	
William Mead	do.	
Andrew McMahan		
Thomas McLain		
Lester Morris	June 7, 1832	
James Norsworthy		
John Nixon		
Julius Nucum		
John Price	do.	
Thomas Poore		
John Parr		
Molliston Perrigin		
Thomas Parker	do.	
Julius Rutherford	March 1, 1823	
Willoughby Rogers	do.	
Samuel Reeves	do.	
Maximilian Rector	do.	
Reuben Roberts	do.	
Samuel Sarrett		
Timothy Sexton	do.	
James Simons	do.	
William Stewart	do.	
Robert Singleton		
John Thomas		
Samuel Tarver	do.	
Richard Walker	do.	
George Woolf		
Jesse Woodroof	do.	
Meshach Willis		
William Willis		
Zebedee Williams		
John Walker, 2d	June 7, 1832	
Archibald Young	do.	

[Doc. No. 127.]   101

PENSIONERS in Indiana who have been dropped under the act of 1st May, 1820; prepared in conformity with a resolution of the House of Representatives of the United States of the 17th December, 1835.

Names.	Acts under which restored.	Remarks.
John Byrd	March 1, 1823	
John Chambers	do	
John Field		
Jonah Frisbie		
William Goben	do	
George Guess		
William Grace		
John Grinstead	do	
Job Hamblin	do	
Philip Hobaugh	do	
Arthur Johnson	do	
Daniel Kenny		
Francis Lucas		
Kimbrow Landres		
John Legore	do	
Hugh Montgomery	do	
Jesse McKensey		
Alexander Monroe	do	Relinquished for an increase of stipend under act 7th June, 1832.
James Jeffrey Murphey		
James Mahoney		
William Overlin	May 15, 1828	
Zebulon Pike	March 1, 1823	Relinquished for an increase of stipend under act 15th May, 1828.
David Porter		
John Pritchett	do	
Hugh Parks	June 7, 1832	
John Pennetent	March 1, 1823	
Benjamin Peachy	do	
Howard Putnam		
Samuel Reeves	do	
Stephen Rodgers	do	
Peter Saurman	do	
John Andrew Smith	do	
Samuel Stone		
David Stilwell		
Evan Thomas	June 7, 1832	
Smith Turner	March 1, 1823	
William Thomas		
Christopher Trinkle		
Peter Vandeventer		
Cornelius Westfall	do	
Obadiah Walker	May 15, 1828	
James Wheeler	June 7, 1832	

PENSIONERS in the State of Illinois who have been dropped from the pension roll under the act of the 1st of May, 1820; prepared in conformity with the resolution of the House of Representatives of the 17th of December, 1835.

Names.	Acts under which restored.	Remarks.
John Cotton		
Clement Edelin	March 1, 1823	
Joseph Evans	do.	
Robert Fisk	do.	
Zachariah Robertson	do.	

PENSIONERS in the State of Mississippi who have been dropped from the pension roll under the act of May 1, 1820; prepared in conformity with the resolution of the House of Representatives of the 17th of December, 1835.

Names.	Acts under which restored.	Remarks.
James Burns		
John Colter	March 1, 1823	
William Clower	do.	
John Fade	do.	
Benjamin Goodwin	do.	

PENSIONERS in the Territory of Michigan who have been dropped from the pension roll under the act of May 1, 1820; prepared in conformity with the resolution of the House of Representatives of the 17th of December, 1835.

Names.	Acts under which restored.	Remarks.
Samuel Stone	May 15, 1828	
Thomas Whipple	March 1, 1823	

[Doc. No. 127.] 103

PENSIONERS in the State of Louisiana who have been dropped from the pension roll under the act of May 1, 1820; prepared in conformity with the resolution of the House of Representatives of the 17th of December, 1835.

Names.	Acts under which restored.	Remarks.
Hampton Stroud	March 1, 1823	

PENSIONERS in Missouri who have been dropped from the pension roll under the act of 1st May, 1820; prepared in conformity with the resolution of the House of Representatives of the 17th December, 1835.

Names.	Acts under which restored.	Remarks.
Uriah Brock		
Peter Rockey Feller	March 1, 1823	
David Strickland	do.	
Thomas Wyatt		

www.ingramcontent.com/pod-product-compliance
Lightning Source LLC
Chambersburg PA
CBHW072202160426
43197CB00012B/2485